Gummy Bears From Hell

Reviews by the people who ate the sugar-free devil spawns…

and lived.

Gummy Bears From Hell
Gary Zenker

Some of the original reviews have been edited for clarity, grammar or spelling so that the writers didn't look completely illiterate. Some specific product names have been genericized. Headlines may have been changed.

We are not responsible for any remaining brand name products or companies that reviewers dragged into this…sh*t. They remain copyright, trademark or whatever of their respective owners, such as they are.

This contains material that is believed to be in the public domain and/or used under fair use guidelines. If you feel otherwise, please contact the publisher with proof so it can be removed from future printings.

No part of this publication may be reproduced, stored in a retrieval system, or transmitted in any format by any means electronic, mechanical, photocopying, recording or otherwise, without the written permission of the author.

Front cover photo courtesy of
Back cover photo courtesy of
Cover and interior: Gary Zenker

Names: Zenker, Gary, Compiler
Title: Gummy Bears From Hell / {compiled by} Gary Zenker
Identifiers: ISBN 978-1-941028-47-6

White Lightning Publishing, Exton, PA

This collection copyright ©2022 Gary Zenker

INTRODUCTION

Product development is an involved and complicated process. It often involves a lot of trial and error, as well as extensive customer testing. Even so, sometimes, the product you design doesn't work quite the way you planned. Sometimes it works better. And sometimes, it offers a completely different…benefit.

One example is that of Dr. Spenser Silver. Working for 3M in the late 1960s, Dr. Silver was working to develop a new strong adhesive. What he discovered was quite the opposite…a low tack, reusable, pressure-sensitive adhesive. Nothing like what he or his company set out to find.

Some might have considered his work a failure and discarded the new adhesive as a result. In fact, 3Ms first reaction to the new adhesive were less than welcoming. It wasn't until 1978 and numerous unsuccessful trials that 3M distributed the adhesive on small pieces of paper for free that the product gained traction. The product was rolled out across the United States in April 1980 and internationally a year later. The rest, as they say, is history. A happy ending, if you will. Not all are.

Which brings me to gummy bears. This happy sweet treat originated in Germany in 1920 using gum Arabic as the original base ingredient. They later developed into Haribo's world-famous Gold Bears candy in 1967.

Somewhere down the line, the company got the idea that a sugar-free version would attract a different market for these sweet-looking bears and be ideal for people who needed to reduce or caloric their sugar intake. Sounds smart so far, right?

But the devil is always in the details.

The product development team needed to select an artificial sweetener to use. They chose maltitol, a sugar alcohol. It, like many wood alcohol ingredients, contains half the calories that sugar does. It so happens that this particular sweetener is also a very effective laxative, even when taken in low quantities. Like the equivalent of seven or eight gummy bears. And honestly, who eats just five or six? We grab those gummy bears by the handful. So you can probably see where this is going. A less than happy ending for people who sample these treats.

Given the figurative and literal tidal waves that resulted from eating the bears, you might expect most people to be upset and angry. Some probably were. But never underestimate the capability of humans to find the silver lining in a dark cloud. The public used the opportunity to spotlight their writing skills and regaled us with tales of their "slice of life" exploits while under the influence.

For anyone who believes that America is completely illiterate, these reviews prove just the opposite: America has a great ability to communicate intelligently about anything it feels important, even if their grammar leaves something to be desired.

The company responsible for the original product has since stopped marketing the product. With the discontinuance of the product in five-pound bags, the archived reviews have sadly all but disappeared.

But the original reviews were too good to be erased from the human consciousness with a simple wave of an electronic eraser. After all, you know the saying: *those who forget history are doomed to repeat it.* So, as a public service, we have rescued a number of them for your enjoyment. These reviews are almost as tasty as the original gummy bears themselves. And if you laugh hard enough at the reviews, well, this book may have some of the same side-effects that the sugarless bears did.

This time at least you were warned in advance.

THE REVIEWS

Gummy Bears From Hell

See you in hell, Sugar-Free Gummi Bears

It was my last class of the semester, and the final exam was worth 30% of our grade. After a late-night study session, I felt confident, but I had to decide between sleeping in or cooking breakfast. My eyelids chose sleep.

My stomach later regretted this decision, and after several uncomfortable stomach growls, I finally decided to make a quick stop by the campus bookstore and grab a snack before my test. Since the semester was ending and everyone was going home for the summer, a lot of items were on sale, including the snacks and candy that they kept up front. Being in the hungry state that I was in, it felt only logical to pick the largest, yet least expensive candy in order to get more bang for my buck.

And there they sat: two bags of Sugar-Free Gummi Bears, buy one get one free.

"What a deal!" I thought naïvely. I would eat one bag before my test, and one bag afterward.

As I walked to class, I gleefully chewed on those abominable little bastards, unaware of the utter mayhem that they would soon unleash upon my poor, poor anus.
I sat down at my desk as the professor informed us that, due to issues with cheating in the past, restroom breaks would be prohibited until the completion of the exam.

"I'll give you 10 minutes to use the restroom now; this will be your last chance. Any takers?"

The demon bears hadn't released their unholy necromancy upon my stomach yet, so in my moment of ignorant foolishness, I remained seated, still munching on those miniature bear-shaped bombs.

After the students wise enough to take the professor's offer had returned, the professor handed out the test. I was six questions in when it happened.

It started subtly at first, almost like a slight tingly sensation in my lower abdomen. I thought nothing of it, assuming my intestines were just doing their thang. Little did I know that my intestines were trying desperately to warn me of the horror that was on the horizon.

By question 9 it happened again, but this time it was followed by a sharp pain, as if those infernal hellions had orchestrated an attack upon my colon. I fought to contain the groan that tried escaping my lips. It was at this point I began to panic; something was going horribly wrong, and I needed to get through this test before it got any worse.

By question 14 my worst fear was upon me; the Satan bears' burning, hot, liquidy dark magic crashed against my anal sphincter like a tidal wave. I was able to close the hatch just in time, but those relentless, toxic bears beat against it like Orcs breaking down the doors of Helm's Deep. I knew I wouldn't be able to so much as shift in my seat without risking a breach.

I kept fighting through my exam, clenching my cheeks with all my might. Beads of sweat began rolling down my neck. Suddenly, a loud, gurgling war cry came from my belly, and the entire class lifted their heads.

At this point, nothing mattered except expelling this ungodly presence from my bowels. With 15 questions left, I promptly wrote C for every answer and ran out of the classroom. My professor yelled something, but I was too preoccupied with the volcanic eruption that needed to take place before I could find sweet, sweet relief.

I burst into the restroom like the Kool-Aid man and, behold, the handicap stall was empty. Sun rays from the adjacent window shone upon it, as if it were a gift from God himself. It took me less than .5 seconds to undo my belt buckle, pull down my pants, and finally relax my weary buttocks upon the toilet seat.

It took absolutely no effort to expel this demon. Almost immediately, the floodgates of hell were opened and the damned, liquified souls of an entire bag's worth of gummi bears cried as they burned through my sphincter and into the watery abyss below. I had never felt such simultaneous relief and anguish in my life.

After 30 more minutes of this, I immediately went home, dug a hole in my backyard, and burned the remaining bag of gummi bears.

Gummy Bears From Hell

I leave with this; do not, and I repeat, do NOT eat these spawns of Satan. Not only did they cause me to fail my final test, but the anguish I experienced is something I wouldn't wish upon anyone, not even my worst enemy. The only place these god-forsaken hell bears belong is buried deep below the Earth's surface.

Worth it

I picked up a bag before the movie. An hour and 20 mins later I had a poopsplosion!! I definitely am gonna buy again! The best tasting laxative I've ever had!

It's All True

If you would like to know what it feels like to be stabbed 30 times in the stomach without dying, or just want to experience the longest and loudest flatulence your body can produce, this is the product for you.

And they're pretty tasty, too.

You don't understand.

I was glued to the toilet seat. Streams of fire burst from my colon. When I wasn't experiencing Satan's fury exploding from my rear, I was laying in the fetal position on my bathroom floor sobbing and asking for forgiveness. I'm a 280 pound man. I. Was. Sobbing.

When it was finally over, I couldn't move. I crawled onto the floor one last time and sat, motionless, until my dehydration finally required that I drink water. The other reviews are perfectly accurate. This is absolutely 100% true.

Eat two at a time. Three if you're brave. But for the love of God and all things on this earth, DO NOT EAT ANY MORE.

The reviews are true.

I gave this a three-star review only due to the bathroom breaks I had to take. The stories are true. For the love of God, listen to the other reviews.

Just eat a few and you should be ok, but after about 6 or so forget it. May the Lord have mercy on your soul. It first starts with flatulence like you went to a Mexican festival and only ate beans. So long and loud that it sounds like you have a percussion band trying to play their hearts out. The problem is it is coming out of you and you alone.

The next stop is the bathroom. It hits you so fast that you need to run like the Flash to the bathroom. Forget walking or jogging. If you have a walker, forget it: I hope you bought Depends. Run like you are racing Superman to the bathroom and that your life depends on it.

When you are finished it feels like you left a piece of your soul and finally got rid of your baby food from the day you were born.

This will probably be the last of me.

This impulse purchase is about to lead to my demise. I have not left the bathroom in 10 hours. I am scared. Send help. I never intended to buy these… I just wanted normal gummy bears. This isn't even my bathroom. Im staying at my new boyfriend's place. this isn't good. pray. pray hard for me. there is not enough Charmin Ultra Soft in the world for me.

Goodbye world.

PS. These are actually quite delicious and I would recommend them to a friend

Gummy Bears From Hell

The Gummy Bear cleanse

Another reviewer said it best, "Oh man...words cannot express what happened to me after eating these. The Gummi Bear cleanse."

First of all, for taste, I would rate these a 5. So good. Soft, true-to-taste fruit flavors like the sugar variety...I was a happy camper.

BUT (or should I say BUTT) not long after eating about 20 of these, all hell broke loose. I had a gastrointestinal experience like nothing I've ever imagined. Cramps, sweating, bloating beyond my worst nightmare. I've had food poisoning from some bad shellfish and that was almost like a skip in the park compared to what was going on inside me.

Then came the, uh, flatulence. Heavens to Murgatroyd, the sounds, like trumpets calling the demons back to Hell...the stench, like 1,000 rotten corpses vomited. I couldn't stand to stay in one room for fear of succumbing to my own odors.

But wait; there's more. What came out of me felt like someone tried to funnel Niagara Falls through a coffee straw. I swear my sphincters were screaming. It felt like my delicate starfish was a gaping maw projectile vomiting a torrential flood of toxic waste. 100% liquid. Flammable liquid. NAPALM. It was actually a bit humorous (for a nanosecond) as it was just beyond anything I could imagine possible.

IT WENT ON FOR HOURS. I felt violated when it was over, which I think might have been sometime in the early morning of the next day. There was stuff coming out of me that I ate at my wedding in 2005.

I had FIVE POUNDS of these innocent-looking delicious-tasting HELLBEARS so I told a friend about what happened to me, thinking it HAD to be some type of sensitivity I had to the sugar substitute. In spite of my warnings and graphic descriptions, she decided to take her chances and take them off my hands.

Silly woman. All of the same for her and a phone call from her while on the toilet (because you kinda end up living in the bathroom for a spell) telling me she really wished she would have listened. I think she was crying.

Her sister was skeptical and suspected that we were exaggerating. She took them to work, since there was still 99% of a 5-pound bag left. She works for a construction company, where there are builders, roofers, house painters, landscapers, etc. Lots of people who generally have limited access to toilets on a given day. I can't imagine where all of those poor men (and women) pooped that day. I keep envisioning men on roofs, crossing their legs and trying to decide if they can make it down the ladder, or if they should just jump.

If you order these, best of luck to you. And please, don't post a video review during the aftershocks.

Beware

Make sure you have plenty of reading material after ingesting these little Satan bears. Even sleep doesn't stop them from making a hot steaming stream of lava out of your backdoor seeing as I'm writing this at 1 am.

If you don't hear from me by 7 am, tell my family I love them. I should have read the reviews and questions before buying! Amateur move, never again

Gummy Bears From Hell

Seems like a nice purchase…

I purchased these "Gummy Bears" thinking "Sounds like a nice purchase: 5 pounds of delicious candy for a decent price. It can't go wrong." Unfortunately I had to learn the hard way.. IT CAN GO VERY WRONG!!

First of all, I made the mistake of not reading the reviews before my purchase, and that is a mistake I will live with for the rest of my life due to the trauma I received after eating two handfuls of these. I was excited to try these for the first time and I will say this: they were surprisingly tasteful for being "Sugar-Free." Regretfully, I decided to try two handfuls within 5 minutes before I had to make a run to Walmart to purchase a few things that didn't include a stockpile of toilet paper.

Within 15 minutes of consuming these high-powered laxatives, my stomach was making noises that I should have seen as a message from God warning me, "You should turn back around and go home." I excused the funny feeling in my stomach, as I was on a mission to replace a Keurig machine. As I parked my car, I felt my stomach growing more agitated by the minute, making gurgling noises that struck me as unusual, but I proceeded into the store as I really wanted a new coffee machine…

GOD HELP ME.

I was literally in the middle of the store looking at small kitchen appliances before one loud gurgle followed another. Then I squeezed out a fart that began as a long squeak and moved to a jet propulsion in a split second that probably some people in the store confused with the sound of a gunshot and probably had some of them ducking for cover.

As my situation had just gone from a 3 on a 1-10 scale (I might need to use the bathroom at some point, I should make this trip quick) to an instant 12 (I'm literally soiling myself in the middle of a Walmart with hand towels and shower towels as my only source of fabric to wipe my ass with). I said "F*** the Keurig," ditched my cart, and went running to the bathroom at the opposite end of the store while what sounded and felt like I had firecrackers exploding in my underwear. People were probably pointing at me while their kids were laughing and I finally made it to the bathroom to find one stall available...the handicapped stall.

Upon entering the bathroom stall while simultaneously crying and pulling my pants down, I jumped on the toilet seat not realizing it was covered in urine. As I began opening the flood gates, releasing the evil that moments prior had begun rearranging my insides, I realized after-the-fact that there was no seat paper. I began holding on for dear life while begging God to kill me, sounding off gunshots out of my ass that most likely had people running out of the store.

USE THIS PRODUCT AT YOUR OWN RISK AND ASK YOURSELF, "WAS IF WORTH IT?" If the answer is yes, you should seek a mental health professional.

I'm pretty sure I lost a kidney

I nearly shat myself inside-out. Pretty sure I crapped out a kidney. I definitely heard the distinctive "ching" of that penny I swallowed back in 1982. And I can now fit back into the pants I wore in High School. So not too bad, I suppose.

Stomach Pain!

They smell and taste amazing, but after having just 10 gummy bears, my stomach was so distended I looked pregnant again. It caused major gas and other stomach issues. It's been a miserable day. But on the plus side, my farts smell like gummy bears. So, now I'm a Unicorn.

Gummy Bears From Hell

Not for the faint of heart

To be honest, I was apprehensive about the validity of these bear's anus-destroying thunder but buckle up if you dare to try these beasts.

On the day I chose to try them, I mistakenly and misfortunately had to leave the cave in which I live. I had eaten only a few (because I was aware of the impending lower intestinal threat) and not five minutes out the door, I felt a rumble that I can only assume would rival the earthquake caused by the Yellowstone volcano.

My guts began to twist and turn as I drove…then silence. I thought it might be over. If only. Moments later another growl so loud that I may as well have been screaming heavy metal rock music to myself in the car exploded in my belly. I feared that a surprise pregnancy may have formed spontaneously in my stomach, but nay.

I rushed to pull over as I felt the overwhelming need to release a brown boy into the small, porcelain sea. I found a gas station and against my better judgment, sacrificed my morals and pulled into the parking lot!

As a hobbled toward the door, my body gargled in distress. My rearward loins spurted gas that could have swept a horse-sized tumbleweed in Kansas. I thought in that desperate moment about how my memoir would end if these beasts inside my bowels took me at that moment. "A loving friend was taken from us too soon, my gummy babies from hell. God bless us and damn those colorful bears."

Gah. I could not end that way. With this in mind, I quickened my pace to a fastidious waddle, all attention focused on reaching the white thrown. The gas station worker eyed me with concern. I looked away embarrassed as another butt-gust escaped me. Ironic that my gas was harboring in such a gastric place.

I practically ripped open the bathroom door and dove toward the flusher. My instincts were abandoned and I released what can only be described as a self-induced butt flood. Not a brown boy. No. An amalgamation of liquidus eruptions with wind speeds of 85 mph or above. And this continued for at least the time it takes a grandparent to argue about the senior soda prices at your local fast-food chain.

After the loudest and may I say spiritual experience of my lifetime, I gracefully wiped my ass and prayed to FDR that my intestines were still attached to my body.

New Deal? I say deal with reality and brand these bears as fanatical laxatives.

In closing, 4/5 overall experience. I wanted to say 3/5 but, honestly, I've never been closer to God than in those moments and this product is not for the faint of heart.

Use with extreme caution or don't eat at all

It is all true eat with extreme caution. I ate about 28 of these death Bear's and I felt okay for about 2 hours and then I thought the grim reaper himself went up my rectum. It felt like I was giving birth to watermelons every 30 minutes for about 9 hours.

Please, for the love of God, don't eat these death Bear's!!!!!!

Gummy Bears From Hell

Ideal April Fool's prank

Bought these to prank some of my friends this year on April Fool's Day. These are sugar-free, and mind you, that means they cause AWFUL diarrhea which was, of course, the whole reason I paid $30 for six small bags of sugar-free gummy bears. They said they were delicious and found it funny when I told them if they ate one, they'd be doomed. Ha ha, good times.

Update:
I gave one bag to my boss and he set it next to his boss' desk. This was probably the most fun I've ever had at work in years. The people that ate them were in the bathroom aaaaallllll day. One guy even stayed late so his relief could use the bathroom.

Definitely recommended for the hilarity of pranking people. Do not get these because you're a diabetic or on a diet. This is not meant to be consumed for anything other than to s*** your pants. And yes, they will make you s*** yourself and then some. Use with great caution.

Sugar-Free Loving

I should add my review after my partner's date with the Bears, the Powder Room downstairs will never be the same. The first wave (which lasted, I kid you not, an entire hour) did so much damage, that the room still is unapproachable. He cleaned the walls, the toilet, and the floor A/C register (out of fear something got down there). Matter of fact, the damage was so bad, he repainted the entire room hoping it would fix "the problem."

BUT IT DIDN'T! The byproduct of the little bears visit was nuclear, the residue will last a lifetime I fear. Oh and it gets better. The other night, he again ate a fist full before we went to get sushi, thankfully at a restaurant I don't really like. Act II, more clean-up and a mandate that we will never go back to that restaurant! That was the best money I have ever spent.

A day that will live in infamy

April 25, 2014 - A day that will live in infamy – I was suddenly and deliberately attack by these evil gummy bears

It all started the day prior when my sugar tooth persuaded me to eat 2 handfuls of these sugar-free delights.

Fast forward 15 hours 23 minutes and 44 seconds, the world shook. All hell broke loose inside me, a sudden headache, my skin began to perspire and something tore around in my abdomen with force enough to make me latch onto my couch with both hands and let out a sheer cry that sent my dog retreating into the bedroom. She probably knew the battle was already lost. I tried to make for the bathroom but the pressure was so intense that I had to wait it out on the couch until a lapse in the gut-busting occurred and I regained control of my muscles. It took only moments before the volcano Mount Anus had blown its top.

The air quickly turned poisonous from the methane and sulfuric fumes that spewed forth. Violence and terror are understatements of what happened for the next 45 minutes. I sustained 3rd-degree burns from contact with the lava that flowed abruptly from my bowels, my blood pressure was at record levels, and my body mass was reduced by 4 lbs.

After ample ventilation of the crime scene, I quickly took a shower and changed clothes because the powerful fumes had soaked through the fabric and into the skin. I almost had a mental breakdown in the shower after realizing those little gummy bears had nearly defeated such a man that I thought I was. I can now hardly bare to look forward through the night-terrors and PTSD that will come of this horrid event...

These little gummies should be made with little horns on their heads. These bears look so sweet and innocent, yet they have an evil side which is equivalent to eating 100 EXLAX tablets!

Gummy Bears From Hell

Backfire

To be quite honest, I read the reviews, and after reading about someone else needing a seatbelt because they gave you so much gas, or about the guy that said to eat these and go on a long road trip if you want to break up with your girlfriend, I just had to try them!! :) The guy that mentions NAPALM is exaggerating a little bit. He must've had a few Jalapeños, or some Mexican food before eating these because they don't put off any heat at all. However, they do everything else others say they do!

I really purchased these bad boys to give to a few CHOICE "friends" and some fellow co-workers! I handed these little guys out like they grew from a tree! I made sure not to give them any more than 15. If you give someone a handful of 30 or more, they may eat only 5 or 10 of them, and save the rest for later. If you give them 15, they are practically guaranteed to eat all 15! So, after handing them out, I sat down at my desk and waited!! ;) These little devils got hold of my co-workers after 45 minutes to an hour and a half, and I have to tell you, I've never had so much fun at work before! There are 5 restrooms in my entire building. There are about 60 people in the building. 1 co-ed restroom, and 2 male/ 2 female restrooms. There was a line of people using the restrooms, even after the guys decided that it was ok to use the female restrooms for EMERGENCY use only!!

BELIEVE ME, THIS WAS AN EMERGENCY!!

My Boss decided he couldn't wait in line, and took off at 10:00 for an early lunch, just so he could use a restroom I think! Let me just say, we have flexible lunch schedules, although we typically limit them to about an hour. He didn't come back until 2:30 and he was not happy! He asked me what I gave him, and I told him that I had just received the package from Amazon (I showed him the box) and that they were sugar-free Gummy Bears! I asked him if he liked them. He said he thought he had a bad reaction to them, but I told him I doubted it since I ate several myself, and nothing happened. (I actually hadn't eaten ANY - I'm so EVIL!!!)

I was in for it though, after he talked to several other people that had the same reaction! They all came into my office at the same time and confronted me about the gummy bear incident! I thought for sure they were going to shove a handful down my throat to see if I had the same reaction, but gladly they didn't!! I have to say I was a bit worried! They all came to the same conclusion, that the gummies were evil and that they needed to be destroyed!! They took them from me, (even after some pleading from me) and destroyed them! By destroying them, I mean of course that they flushed them down the toilet, to send them to the horrible place that had just claimed 4 days worth of bowel movements from each person!!!

So, after going through only about 10% of a 1 pound bag, I have to say it was worth every bit!! Needless to say, I have now ordered a 5 pound bag, so I can give them to my "choice" friends (seeing as I wasn't quite able to distribute them after the first incident) and post another fun bit in the 5 lb section! :)

If you are looking to eat these as treats, take my word for it and just buy the regular sugar gummies. A few cavities wont hurt as bad as these little devils will! If you want to put the HURT on to a couple of "choice" people, by all means, these are the gummies for you!! :)

It's been a rough couple of years for my family. There have been a few land disputes, some nasty feuds, several imprisonments and a beheading. But perhaps our most celebrated misfortune was what has come to be known as The Brown Wedding.

I don't want to bore you with all the details, but essentially my cousin Robb was betrothed to the daughter of a family rival. Then, against all our counsel, he eloped with another woman. Classic Robb.

Anyway, you can imagine our surprise when we found ourselves invited to the wedding of the jilted bride. Perhaps it should have been a red flag. But we Starks love a free meal, so off we went.

They threw it in their castle. After a tense exchange between Robb and the father of the bride, the ceremony was performed, and we all sat down for the feast. It was bench seating. The food was simple fare--beans, broccoli, and bran muffins. Again, a warning sign, but we were caught up in the merriment and the wine.

Dessert arrived. The waiters uncovered tureens filled with colorful piles of gummy bears--a welcomed note of levity. The fifes played a jig, and we all dug in. They were delightful--fruity and delicious.

Gummy Bears From Hell

Twenty minutes later, the father of the bride proposed a toast. "To the Starks," he said. "May all your misfortunes be behind you."

Around this time, I began to feel uncomfortable rumblings down below, and looked about for a restroom. As my eyes scanned the hall, I noticed that the bride's family weren't eating the gummy bears. A waiter was refilling the tureen next to me. I snuck a glance at the bag—sugar-free Gummy Bears. My blood ran cold.

I rose to shout a warning to my family, but the alarm came from my backside--a three-note trumpet blast that ended badly. I felt a fullness in the back of my pants. A thousand shocked eyes turned to me. And then the room erupted in a cacophony of flatulence--and worse. Far worse.

How can I describe it? The sights, the sounds, the smells. And the pain--like a grappling hook dragged backward through my bowels.

I watched in horror as, one by one, my family doubled over succumbing to the ceaseless waves of stabbing pain. Some were clutching their bellies, others lay writhing on the floor or stumbling in circles, emitting auburn plumes of effluvium. The walls were soon spattered with our suffering.

The father of the bride watched it all with intent eyes, delighted by the macabre spectacle.

I saw Robb--brave Robb--fall victim to the gastronomic assault. Not even his pregnant wife was spared. Monstrous.

Soon only our matriarch was left standing, teetering as she made a final plea for mercy. But too late. She fell to her knees and erupted, and what came out of her haunts me to this day.

So hear me and hear me well. I swear vengeance on them, their house and their kin. I will hunt them to the last of their line, from Winterfell to Casterly Rock. And if I do not live to see their castle burn to the ground, I will at least light the match. For, by the gods, someone needs to light a match in that place.

Ode to the bear of gummy

The bear glows like a nuclear plant
It's little head is something to see
A burst of wonderful flavor,
And it looks like I've eaten them all, just me.

My stomach is growling like a swirling storm inside
Couldn't keep it in, heaven knows I tried!

Don't let them in, don't eat them all
Be the strong person you always have to be
One or two, but no more than three, don't let them in
Well, now they're in!

Let it blow, let it blow
Can't hold it inside anymore
Let it blow, let it blow
Grab the throne and slam the door!

I don't care
What they're going to tear
Let the storm rage on,
With the other gummi's, there was nothing to fear

It's funny how your hunger
Makes everything seem small
And the bears that once controlled me
Can't get to me at all!

It's time to see what I can do
To eat the whole bag and just break through
Yellow, Red or Green, no rules for me

Let it blow, let it blow
I'm holding on to the sides
Let it blow, let it blow
This sounds like the rush of big water park slides

Here I sit
And here I'll stay

Gummy Bears From Hell

Let the storm rage on!

The power of the smell flurries through the air into the house
My stomach is spiraling in gummi fractals causing me to dowse
And one thought crystallizes as I tighten and start to blast
I'm never going back to the bag,
These gummi's just don't last.

Let it blow, let it blow
And I'll rise like a brand new man
Let it blow, let it blow
A sugar free bear just ran!

Here I stand
But just when I thought it had ended
Another storm is raging on,
These damn bears have me expended

Again I sit
And here I'll stay
I can't take the pressure
And I'm out of Lysol spray!

You will hurt

I got some of these in my stocking for Christmas. I guess Santa hates me. It hurt. It still hurts. I just got over the flu and now this? I didn't realize that it was the gummies, until coming across a meme online. I found the culprit. Three is too many. Way too many.

Cast iron no more

First off, let me start by saying that I used to pride myself on having a cast iron stomach. Keywords USED TO. These little monstrosities initially had no effect, and I was mildly disappointed in my purchase. If there is indeed a hell, that's what my entire digestive system went to a few hours after the fact.

If I had to describe what happened using a song title, it would have to be "Chocolate Rain" by Tay Zonday. Some stay dry, I definitely felt the pain. It felt like World War III had just been declared in my stomach with the amount of gurgling it was doing. Part of me was terrified I was indeed going to die with my pants around my ankles inside a port-a-potty. It was so bad I'm fairly certain the cleaners were going to be gagging in the morning when they came through.

If you're a sick bastard who just feels like you deserve some kind of punishment, this is for you. You WILL think about everything bad you've ever done in your life while praying for sweet merciful Death to tell you it's over. I wasn't just reunited with the gum from 3rd grade, I was reunited with the coins I ate in kindergarten. Don't let the generic packaging fool you.

Where to begin? Little did I know my life would be changed forever after eating a bag of these little b@stards! Have you ever prayed for death, but death wouldn't come? My journey began with a bear crawl to the bathroom - because I was unable to stand from the gouging stomach pain!

It was only an approximate 8-foot crawl, but I imagined it was like crawling through the Vietnamese jungle circa 1968. My colon and stomach were at obvious war with the little fun bears I had consumed, there was an 8-hour period where I didn't know which was going to be the victor! My stomach was making sounds like a wounded calf makes in the wild. Well…a wounded calf that was possessed by a demon from hell!! Then the uncontrollable anal vomiting began. The sheer velocity of which these bears were leaving my body would've taken out most men! It was like a Wagner power sprayer hooked up to a hurricane!
Then came the awful disgusting stench. I figured that I had already vacated my bowels tens of thousands of times by this point in my life, and I had never smelled something so inhumane. The closest thing it

Gummy Bears From Hell

resembled was the great jungle gym tire fire of 1987 at a local park I used to play at.

At this point, I had all but given up on life as I crawled into a bathtub full of water to alleviate the crippling stomach pains. I thought about my 2 children, and how they would grow up without a father. A father who was just looking to cut back a little on his sugar intake and be healthy.

Then came the uncontrollable sobbing. It's amazing how emotional a grown man can become after blowing out his anus and half his insides.

Did I mention the smell? If I could bottle that smell, we wouldn't need a border patrol! It would turn back even the most determined illegal immigrant! Forget ISIS and Al Quaeda, the real terrorists are anyone who had a hand in designing, making, distributing, and selling this product. The physical scars may have healed, but I lost a part of me that day 8 years ago that I can never get back!!

After reading these informative reviews, I bought these for my ex as a combination divorce/happy affair gift. You know, as a gesture of post-marital goodwill :) He loves gummy candy and often told me he was popping out to buy some but those store trips would mysteriously take a couple of hours. He just couldn't get enough "Candy" and it eventually ended our marriage.

Thank you for another perfect gift idea!

Hell holds no surprises for me anymore...

This is a cautionary tale and - unlike most of the other reviews on this product - this is a true story and its authenticity can be qualified by a small news item that appeared in the Toronto Star's local news section during the month of April in 2013, much to my chagrin.

I would consider myself a prudent man. Not given to bouts of outspokenness or craving attention, and certainly not one to rock the boat. On any given day I can be found reading a crime novel on a park bench in the middle of the city, soaking in the opulence of nature while nibbling on my tuna fish sandwiches and fending off the voracious gulls and squirrels that threaten to spoil my repose. This is me. Law-abiding and introspective. Which is why it came as a shock to me to find myself incarcerated because of the Devil's Confectionery, Satan's Sweetmeat, Lucifer's Lozenges - the horror that is known as sugar-free Gummy Bears.

I'll set the scene: It was late winter / early spring in Toronto and the city had just been digging itself out from a lalate-seasonnowstorm. I was heading to Pearson International Airport for a redeye flight to Amsterdam in order to give the Dutch arm of our company some training on the new software that had been installed (I'm deliberately being vague to prevent my place of work from being linked in any way to the incident that occurred).

I had just finished packing, checked the time and found I was running late: my flight was at 7:10 PM and it was now almost 5:00 PM. Cursing softly, I ran out to the car and threw my bags in the trunk, hitting the gas a little harder than usual in my haste to make it to the Long-Term Parking Lot as soon as possible. Luckily, traffic was light on the 401 and I made it to the airport in record time, but knew that my chances of making the flight were still at risk if I didn't use my time wisely.

I hadn't eaten since lunch, and I was feeling a bit hungry, my stomach rumbling loudly in protestation, which caused me to look around at the other travelers rushing past me in the busy terminal, mortified that my bodily noises might be heard by others. I briskly checked my watch and decided that I had enough time to grab a quick snack before going through the baggage check and security

Gummy Bears From Hell

and would get something more substantial once I was checked through security.

I spotted a vending machine nestled in a relatively low-traffic corner of the terminal and rushed over, already pulling out my credit card and mentally assessing what I had a craving for so as to save time interacting with the machine. My eyes scanned the colourful array of confection quickly, coming to rest on a tantalizing, rainbow-coloured bag of gummy bears with the simple white and red logo emblazoned across the bag in what appeared to be a slightly tweaked Helvetica Rounded font.

Now I'd to pause here in the story for a moment to underscore the importance of making proper choices. I was hungry. When you're hungry, you should eat FOOD. FOOD is defined as "a nutritious substance that people consume to maintain life", this is what food is. These days, the definition of the word 'food' has been bastardized and the meaning has been broadened to include veritably any material that can be digested, or rather, chewed and swallowed without causing death or severe illness.

Sugar-free Gummy Bears are NOT food. They aren't even from this planet. I imagine their origins being conceived in a boardroom in hell by a top team of Creative Pain Administers, with senior-level Demons rubbing their hands together in ghoulish delight as Hell's Chief Chemist slowly lifts the veil on their new creation.

The point here being I made a very, very, very poor choice. I pushed the button and the vending machine ejected the brightly coloured bag into my awaiting hands. I had always liked gummy bears - they were bright but rather innocuous, they weren't overly sweet so as to become cloying and - of course - each candy came in the visage of a rather happy, docile bear reminiscent of the picture one's mind's eye holds of all anthropomorphic bears from Yogi to Winnie.

The way I figured it, I was taking a bit of a holiday from life, so I could relax my fastidiously regimented daily schedule a little to allow for some frivolity. After all, I was going to be in Amsterdam come morning with 16 hours to kill before I had to be training the Dutch employees, maybe I would take a trip down to one of the Coffee Shops in the Red-Light District and really let my hair down! No, I wouldn't do that. I would see that area of the city from the bus as I went to the hotel where I would eat at the hotel restaurant and drink sparkling water. So I'd better enjoy the gummy bears, my one extravagance to commemorate my break from routine.

I joined the queue in the KLM line, which was mercifully short, most likely because all of the passengers for my flight had already been checked through as the flight was scheduled to depart in an hour. I checked my watch again, frowned, and absent-mindedly opened the bag of "Haribo Sugar-Free Gummy Bears" and began to munch on them as the line slowly advanced. To be fair, they tasted fine - just like every other manufacturer's brand of the colourful candy, and they were sugar-free to boot. This is what made the whole incident that followed so baffling - if they had tasted 'off' or 'different' I most likely wouldn't have continued to shovel them into my mouth absent-mindedly while daydreaming about what I would order to eat from room service in my hotel in Amsterdam.

As I gave the attendant my e-ticket and she weighed my bags, the first of the pains began in my stomach. I thought nothing of it at first, chalking it up to the fact that I needed something more substantial than gummy worms to tackle my hunger. But over the course of the next five minutes, the shooting pain began to come in more rapid succession. At this point, I had my boarding pass printed and rubbing my stomach a little, I proceeded to security. I briefly entertained the thought of trying to find a restroom before going through security, but at that point my discomfort was manageable and I didn't think it would get any worse, certainly not within the amount of time it would take to clear security.

I joined the line and started fishing for my passport to present to the agent checking tickets, I felt a thin sheen of sweat break out on my forehead and underarms, and my features flushed for a moment as a wave of heat washed over me. I didn't pay it much heed as going through security always caused me great anxiety and I chalked it up to pre-flight jitters.

It was only as I stood face to face with the agent and handed her my passport and ticket that I had a glimpse of the agony that was about to begin. It felt like time rippled for a moment, as if my consciousness buckled so intense was the pain that fired through my bowels. I grimaced spastically and emitted a low moan, then felt myself take an involuntary step sideways. Stars shot through my head briefly and my

Gummy Bears From Hell

vision blurred and then snapped back into focus. The agent was staring at me with slight consternation and asked me if I was alright. I pulled myself together, stood up straight and declared that I was fine, mortified that I had had a lapse of decorum not only in public but at the security clearance in an airport!

As I fumbled off my belt to go through the metal detector, the pain in my stomach increased and I practically had to sit on the floor to take my shoes off, terrified of what would happen if I bent at the middle to do it. It was becoming increasingly more evident to me that this wasn't just a stomach ache. No, this was something much worse.

As a child I had had a bout of diarrhea after a trip to Mexico with my family, I remember the feeling of nausea that swept through me before my child-self had surrendered to the gas pains and parked myself on the toilet for an hour, s***ting until I felt like I didn't have any bones left. And that was how I was feeling now, with several key differences - the pain was worse, the sense of an impending bowel movement was so formidable it gave me temporary amnesia, and it took all of my will-power, all of it, to clench my butt cheeks together to prevent my sphincter from exploding.

A sudden shock of pain racked my body, and I half wondered if I was going to give birth to a Tasmanian Devil. The crazy, fever-induced image of said cartoon animal chasing Bugs Bunny through the splashy, volcanic s***-kettle that was my stomach, caused me to illicit a short, maniacal bark of laughter as I approached the Metal detector, a wild, distant look in my eyes, sweat now beginning to poor off of my like a long-distance runner in Kenya.

The security agent on the other side of the detector shot a quick glance over to her co-worker who narrowed his eyes and made a subtle movement towards his holster. My breathing became uneven as I entered the metal detector and I realized with alarm that I had taken off my socks without even registering it, and one of my shirt tails was untucked at the front. I held my breath, my eyes bulging dangerously from my head as the machine scanned me.

As I shakily moved forward towards the agent for a pat down, my stomach began to illicit sounds that can only be described as otherworldly. It started off as a sort-off bubbling sound heard from afar and grew in pitch and intensity at an alarming rate. My jaw dropped in shock as what I can only describe as the sound of an agonized wailing alley-cat in heat with a persistent Doppler effect added to its voice emitted from some nether-region of my intestines.

The officer's eyes widened in alarm, and she kept her eyes glued to my stomach as she thoroughly patted me down. As she reached my shins, I felt my innards suddenly expand, and plummet towards my rectum. With cat-like reflexes I squeezed my sphincter shut with what seemed like nano-seconds to spare, and I knew, I KNEW that if I didn't get to the bathroom immediately I would s*** myself.

With a Herculean effort and all of the strength that I could muster, I forced my butt cheeks together knowing that one false move would open the floodgates. I began to walk like a duck, trying to remain as inconspicuous as possible, not even caring now what other people were seeing in front of them - a disheveled, barefoot 40-year-old businessman, red-faced and bulgy-eyed, sweating profusely, shaking slightly and walking without bending his knees.

With single-minded intensity I grabbed my carry-on, shoes and socks from out of the plastic tub that had passed the x-ray inspection, and without putting anything back on, I turned on my heels with the intention of finding the nearest restroom and slowly dying there one squirt at a time.

But that's not what happened.

I turned to go and found myself staring at three armed agents who stopped me and asked if I would follow them. "Why, what's the matter?" I stammered, wincing slightly as the act of speech seemed to strain the tenuous and extremely fragile truce I had negotiated between my bowels and the tempest that raged within. "I have to go the bathroom, RIGHT NOW" I pleaded. "Just follow us please," they said, leaving no room for argument.

The other travelers clearing the security check stared with curiosity and revulsion at the spectacle unfolding before them, whispering amongst themselves and hurrying to pack up their belongings and get as far away from me as possible, no doubt assuming that the airport had nabbed some sort of domestic terrorist. If I hadn't been feverishly trying to hold back the eruption of Mount Vesuvius, I likely would have died of shame.

Gummy Bears From Hell

With each step I took towards the room that they ushered me into, I felt that my legs would give way. I marveled at how strong the human will could be. Marveled at what was essentially patching a hole in the Hoover Dam with bubblegum could actually be sustained indefinitely. Maybe I would make it through this ordeal after all.

The room they brought me into was an examination room. I had pretty much stopped registering details of my environment as my consciousness closed off all but the absolutely necessary functions - breathing, ability to walk - but I snapped back to reality when I heard the snap of rubber. The slow dawning of realization poked through my agony and stoic resolve as I turned to face an agent dawning rubber gloves.

"Sir, we are going to perform a cavity search on you", a young fresh-faced agent stated in a firm but emotionless voice. His short-cropped, blond hair was immaculate and for one crazy moment I wondered if he was an actor and this was all some sort of elaborate practical joke done to amuse bored kids watching YouTube. He must have taken my tortured silence for resistance because he looked at me sharply and said "Lower your pants and underwear please, and face the desk."

Panic started to grip me in its icy grasp and the sudden adrenaline threatened to destroy my sphincters bulwarks and rend my anus in two. I inhaled sharply and with a pained gasp I doubled up my efforts to clench my cheeks together. "Sir, please", I begged, deferring to this kid in an act of desperation, "I have to go to the bathroom. You can follow me into the stall if you need to but I had some bad sugar-free Gummy Bears" and now I feel like…" but they had stopped listening and smirked at each other, two of the other agents - a tall, dark-haired female and a shorter, balding fat man - looked away from me and I could see them shaking a little as they stifled their laughs. "Sir, face the wall, put your hands on the desk and spread your cheeks," the young agent stated, a lop-sided grin on his face. "But…" I began to protest, and then a fresh shock of pain forced me to stop and lean on the table for support as an ungodly howling rose from my stomach, something between the dying moans of a Wholly Mammoth and the sound of bubble-wrap popping underwater. I exhaled shakily and my focus began to narrow as I rallied for the final battle.

Shaking uncontrollably and sweat literally raining down onto the tabletop in from of me, I turned to face the wall and heard a meek childlike voice, pleading from somewhere in the room. "Please," it said, and then again, "please." From somewhere within me my mind recognized that this sound had issued from me, although my consciousness had now begun to separate from my body and I held my breath and prayed to God for strength.

"He probably has some heroin or something up there that opened up," the female guard said as a part of me that hadn't escaped into the ether yet acknowledged that she was behind me to my left. "Probably high as a kite, LOOK at him," she said. The shorter guard agreed with a snort, off to my right.

"Spread your cheeks," the young agent said, his voice directly behind me and lower than the other two, "and bend over."

"Pleasegodpleasegodpleasegodpleasegod", I whispered in a desperate, maniacal mantra, not even aware of my surroundings anymore. I felt like I was lost in an opium fog with half-snatched images and sounds filtering through to create a nonsensical version of reality. Another volley of pain tore through me and I involuntarily leaned forward over the desk, my focus completely narrowed now to a spot on the wall two feet in front of me, a curious imperfection in the what seemed to be white-washed stone wall. It was a dark blotch about five millimeters long and shaped like a smiling bear, a yellow dancing bear. No, a green bear. No, red. It was all the colors of the rainbow. My god, it was beautiful.

It just took something as simple as a slight breeze to trigger Armegeddon. That's all. No trumpets, no fanfare, no fire raining from the heavens, no dogs and cats living together in harmony, no finger on the button, no prophet to predict it, no nothing. As I stared at the rainbow bear smiling and dancing in front of me, my mouth agape, drooling, eyes glazed and blood-shot, face coated with a sheen of sweat, I heard the softest sound, an exhalation from the young agent behind me, and then at the same instant the warm air of his breath feather across my butt cheeks. For just a moment, maybe less, maybe a split second, even a nanosecond, I felt the presence of God there with me in that room as neurons began to misfire at a blinding rate, nerve endings bristled and muscles twitched reflexively. I stood on the brink with one foot hovering over the edge, and then without

Gummy Bears From Hell

taking a step, I found myself plummeting.

With a sound like an extra-large plastic ketchup bottle being run over by a Mac truck, my sphincter released. The pressure of the blast pushed me hard into the desk and the legs of the desk screeched as they scraped across the floor.

My body remained rigid for a moment and I experienced a relief that can only be described as orgasmic in its purity. My eyes rolled back in my head and my tongue lolled out of my head like a half-retarded dog and I emitted a low, sustained groan that grew in pitch as the filthy torrent pushed its way out of my body. Tremors wracked my body and I must have looked like a fish out of water with an endless stream of s*** firing out of its ass. Other sounds and sensations started to filter in now as my consciousness began to materialize once more.

The muffled scream of a dungeon filled with prisoners near death radiated from my stomach; the rushing sound of litres of liquid trying to escape through an aperture too small to accommodate it all at the same time; the omnipresent sound of chunky liquid spattering against a hard surface with great force; the high-pitched screaming of a woman's voice calling out to God, another voice sobbing uncontrollably imploring to "make it stop!!!" and my own ecstatic, monotone wail.

When my ordeal had eventually run its course, I was left panting for breath and wobbly-legged, half-crying, half-laughing with relief, barely lucid and feeling as if I had birthed an elephant. My colon felt like someone had poured chile sauce all over it and then sent in a colony of fire ants to eat it. Through my sobs I heard the sound of dripping, like when the sprinklers are eventually turned off after an office fire, or after a thunderstorm when the willow that overhangs a pond continues to rain down long after the sky has stopped. From behind me, the sobbing continued and I heard someone trying to speak into a walkie-talkie but nonsensical words were all that the man could speak, which sounded like the ravings of a lunatic.

With great relief, I slowly pulled myself off the table, legs trembling, my stomach eliciting one last sound, a loud prolonged gas bubbling that eerily resembled a pig orgasm. I slowly turned my head to survey the devastation and in that instant, if I had had a pencil or some other sharp object, I probably would have gouged my eyes out in revulsion. And the smell. The smell was enough to drive a man insane. It was the stench of rotting potatoes mixed with sulfur and ammonia, cooked in a broth of chicken feces and left to age for two weeks in a yeasty stew at the bottom of a French outhouse. After half a whiff of this ghoulish brine, I immediately stopped breathing through my nose but the taste was to remain in the back of my throat for months to come.

The young agent had taken the brunt of the foul witch's brew, and at first I couldn't process what I was seeing. I thought somehow the young blond kid had been spirited away and replaced by a brown Golem, or an ATV rider that had spent the better part of a day driving through every mud puddle he could find after a torrential downpour.

With some degree of compartmentalization, I came to understand that for some unfathomable reason this kid hadn't moved - or hadn't been able to move - through the entire fecal deluge. He had weathered the entire assault head-on like some sort of hero from Greek Mythology. I had given this poor schmuck a one-man s*** bukkake that would make a Brazilian pornographer retch with disgust, and he was still in the same position he must have been from the moment of first impact.

I tried to comprehend how he must be feeling, what he must be going through psychologically, but it became evident very quickly that he had become very broken. No doubt forced so deeply within himself once the firehose has been turned on that there was little to no hope of him ever coming back from it, certainly not without extensive psychotherapy or a lobotomy.

I looked beyond his quivering, catatonic crouched form to see a perfect outline of him cutout on the white wall behind him, either side filled in with a dripping, opaque layer of alternately pulpy and runny fecal stew. I noticed two quivering masses at either extreme of the room and realized they were humanoid in form, although the caterwauling that was coming from these broken creatures was just blubbering gibberish. And this was the tableau that was burnt into my mind's eye for eternity.

Needless to say, I missed my flight.

In fact, the next week is a blur. I have vague recollections of an army

Gummy Bears From Hell

of Hazmat-clad figures looming through the brown landscape of the soiled room, the slopping sounds of rubber boats squelching in puddles of fetid detritus, uncontrollable wailing and animal-like sounds issuing from the mouths of creatures that had been traumatized beyond their capacity for being put back together, the complete loss of sensation from my waist down as I was rolled through the room on a waterproof gurney, it's wheels struggling to surf on top of the s***-soaked floor.

I spent a week or so in the hospital enclosed in a well-ventilated, sealed room, with a suited doctor coming in on the hour to monitor my vital signs as they tried to rehydrate my body. I had apparently expelled every available drop of water from my body that was possible to sustain life without for a short period of time. All of my clothes were incinerated in the hospital's crematorium, and the soiled bag of sugar-free Gummy Bears was never recovered.

This is my story. It is inconceivable to think that this kind of product can be sold legally and be misrepresented as 'food'. I was lucky, I survived. But as for the families of the survivors, and the survivors themselves, they will forever live with the trauma of the events that took place at Pearson International Airport on that snowy day in April 2013.

It's all true.. all of it.

I ate 6 of these things to aid along in digestion. I figured it was a tastier way to rid myself of a weeks' worth of backup. I might as well have swallowed a nuclear bomb and topped it off with an enema. The good news is my digestive system is back on track. The bad news is I will never eat another gummy bear and may have flushed part of my soul down the toilet.Godspeed my friends...

The effects are indeed very real

So I read through a lot of the reviews here and decided it might be a fun prank item to buy since I'm an evil human being. I received my 5-pound bag two days after ordering. Now I was somewhat skeptical, especially since my own digestive system is fairly robust. It takes some potent stuff to give me the runs. Some laxatives even have no effect on me.

So I tried them. I ate 5 bears before bed. Woke up. Nothing. Thought to myself "Pfft these are weak" but they do taste amazing. I ate approximately 20 more of them that morning. In less than a half hour, my gut was rumbling. But it was only some gas. Meh. About another half hour passed, then it hit me. Oh boy, it hit hard.

My gut felt like Chuck Norris had reached his hand up my anus and had roundhouse kicked my insides. I made my way to the bathroom with a brisk walk. Sat down on the toilet. It took a few seconds, but then all hell broke loose. I've literally never had diarrhea that explosive before. Kid you not, I sat there through 5 gnarly explosions before the flood gates opened and about a gallon and a half of pure liquid ran out of me.

I'm a firm believer in this product's potential now and I'm bagging up the remainder of my 5 pound bag to give to select friends and family. May even leave a bowl of them in the break room at work.

But they make my ass sound like Chewbacca.

These things are delicious, but they make my ass sound like Chewbacca.

Gummy Bears From Hell

Like distant thunder

It all started at 6 in the morning. The night before one of my hunting buddies had bought these without noticing that they were sugar-free. He's one of those guys always reading about the effects of food and dieting and stuff, and refused to eat them claiming they would make you gain weight.

So he gave them to me. I was out in the deer woods far from any toilet, or toilet paper. If I could go back in time, I would have run my friend over on the way, or made sure my parents had never met, because after just 5 or so of this hell-bent demon-possessed spawn of Satan bears, I knew I should have read the comments before taking these off my friends' hands.

It all started with a low rumble, like distant thunder, or the mating call of a rhinoceros. I was sure it would scare away any deer within a 5-mile radius.

But it didn't stop at that. My intestines began to move inside of me like snakes after eating cherry bombs. My soul itself seemed to be working its way through my bowls. By then I knew I had to get out of that tree stand, but by then I knew it was too late. I made a break for it just as the sun began to rise. I ran like a madman in a way that I can only describe as a pregnant, ostrich sasquatch woman. I had only made it a few yards when Lucifer himself shot out of me like a potato tied to a ceiling fan.

I crumbled to the ground as I tried to rip off my extremely expensive no-scent camouflage hunting pants, but it was too late. I stayed in that spot for what felt like hours. My life flashed before my eyes, and I relived the time I caught my first bass. I prayed to God to kick a satellite from the sky to crush me, but my cries for mercy were covered by the explosions of Satan still coming from my body. The stuff coming out of me would have caught fire if you'd struck a match anywhere near it.
As I sat with my tormented thoughts, I saw the biggest buck I have ever seen in my life (about a 12 or 14 point) walk slowly past my tree stand. A FLIPPEN PURFECT SHOT. I sat in a puddle of my own defeat trying not to suffocate on the fumes coming from the tainted turds.

After what seemed like an eternity, I managed to waddle back to my brand new truck where I had no other clothes, or anything to clean myself with. The smell of my truck and the butt stains left on my once perfect seats will forever torment my dreams. I have gone through an eternity of air fresheners and nothing has worked. Whenever someone has to drive with me and they ask what happened to my truck, I tell them a really long story about how I delivered a calf in the middle of the night.

Night of 1000 waterfalls
Well, I read the reviews...challenge accepted!

Final score - death bears 7...me 0.

You know how amazon gives you things that people also bought with your item...they should include some Cottonelle wipes as a mandatory item with this.

My pre-colonoscopy meds were not as effective as the 40 bears I ate. Why 40 you say? Well, I ate 5 and nothing...10
Nothing. Kept on going. Got a little cocky and ate 10 straight. Now, I'm thinking I've won! 10 more...sure, and 10 more.

It was at this point that i actually read the packaging. It actually says may have a laxative effect.

And here comes the night of a thousand waterfalls.

Don't do the challenge. I thought they were all making stuff up.

Gummy Bears From Hell

Very tasty - Very dangerous

The rumors are true - this product is incredibly tasty. The gummy bears were soft, and they have just the right amount of firmness to them to be satisfying to chew on. The flavor had a little bit of a tang to it, like actual fruit - eating the lemon-flavored bear reminded me of the tangy taste of actual lemon zest. All in all, the physical quality is leagues above half the stuff I bought from stores - their gummies are hard to chew, offer little in the ways of flavor, and end up making me feel sick to my stomach.

However, these bears (like real bears) cannot be taken lightly. The sugar alcohol has a laxative effect - something a family member found out just 3 hours after these arrived at my door. Be warned: this is not a ones-and-donesie affair; if you have more than, say, 20 of these things in one sitting, you had better hope you don't have anything important to do that takes you away from the house (and the bathroom). This is a sunrise to sundown problem. This is something that you will feel for HOURS. Cramping at best; frequent visits to the bathroom at worst. It will keep you up at night. You will be sitting on the toilet at 4 AM wondering where you lost control of your life. I can't stress enough that you have to be careful about how many of these things you eat.

And for people doing a low-carb diet (like the keto diet) remember that this particular sugar alcohol isn't perfect - about 67% of the carbs will get absorbed, so eat lightly! You may honestly be better off buying regular gummy candy and having some self-control.

That being said, in some ways, these gummies are effective if you're doing a low-carb diet, because the laxative effect means that these gummies are self-moderating. You might WANT to eat a lot of them, but the that would ruin your diet - luckily, you learn very quickly that you CAN'T eat a lot of them. It's a problem that solves itself.

Overall, I rate these things 5/5 stars. VERY tasty, VERY fresh, but also VERY dangerous.

These are GOOD FOR LOSING 10 LBS through extreme bowel movements

Worth every cent for April Fools, I bought this these for the guys in my shop. Two other guys that were diabetics knew right away what they were, the rest had no clue. I get them, immediately take them out to the shop and say "here you go guys, I accidentally ordered the sugar-free. Have at them."

Immediately Clint starts eating them with no effects until after he leaves work, I hear it is date night so he goes out to eat with his wife. He spends the whole dinner in the bathroom, he finally received a text saying I paid for the food I'm out in the car waiting, he spent his whole dinner on the toilet. Even on the way back to town he must stop and use their toilet again.

On Monday I find all this out, he thinks it was only bad McDonald's. He continues to eat them on Monday, along with Eric who was absent Friday. Hilarity ensues! The two have handfuls and handfuls. After lunch, I hear Eric saying he spent his whole lunch on the toilet and nothing but water is coming out! He tells me this as he's waiting for the bathroom in the shop. I asked him if he ate the gummies. He says yes, and I laughed so hard my cheeks hurt. He immediately knows what was up.

At that moment Clint walks out the bathroom, and we both asked him if he's ate the gummies also, he says yes also. I laughed so hard I cried. He still doesn't understand why. I finally tell them that the sugar-free kind act as laxatives. Both immediately hate me. It's days later and my cheeks still hurt from laughing so much. As I watch Clint work for the rest of the day, I see he cannot so much as lift 5 pounds without the fear of farting or should I say sharting. He moves his work slowly inch by inch, panting heavily after every move. I can see it in his face he hates me so much.

Eric on the other hand tells me he spends all day with his ass cheeks sweating, and his belly gurgling. By the end of the day it burns to poop. The rest of the guys tell me I see Clint and Eric fighting over the bathroom and at times prancing like a horse waiting for their turn.

After this happened, we warn Austin. Unaffected by the 5 he ate on Friday, he tries to be a badass and takes a handful and stuff them into his mouth. He is unaffected until that evening. He lives in a duplex next to another coworker with very thin walls. The co-worker tells me he can hear him all night long farting like a trumpet and yelling out "F*** you, I'm going to get you back."

This is been the best money I've spent in a long time. And I still have half a bag left.

Ever want to be the Michelin Man?

How about the Stay Puff Marshmellow man? Those dreams are about to be reality when you buy these little treats!

As no doubt you've read, it doesn't take much to elicit the cascade of death. But try 2 handfuls and you will easily cleanse your entire digestive track in about 8 hours, more efficiently and effectively then anything short of disembowelment.

You may want to record the next few hours as you will be a human balloon that is full of so much air, if you stop farting you will explode in a fashion so spectacular, Watson the super-computer won't be able to figure out where your atoms are.

Unless becoming a human bomb is on your bucket list, you probably should just eat the regular gummy bears. I will be serving them to my friends at our next poker function.

The results are noxious and disgusting. Use at your own risk, and be prepared for a fate worse than death.

You do realize that these 'sugar-free' bears have the exact same calories as the regular Haribo gummy bears!

I foolishly ignored the warnings and purchased a 5 pound bag of these potent evil apparitions posing as delectably tasty goodies.

The laxative effect of these 'sugar free gummy candies' is nuclear. I first noticed rumblings as my intestines began a protest that escalated to world-shaking levels. The gurgling and surging was grotesque. They continued to increase in both intensity and duration until the volume alerted all in the house of my impending explosion. Sphincter tightly clenched I urgently made the most awkward hurried hobbling walk to the bathroom. I arrived just barely in time as the propulsion physically lifted me forcefully off the seat of the commode. Without being able to grasp and maintain butt to commode seat integrity, I shudder to wonder the scope of destruction of the resulting explosiveness.

The stench quickly overcame the exhaust fan, passive air freshener, aerosol spray, and tightly closed door. It was beyond awful. To save others in the house from a fate worse than death, I waddling to the door between liquid explosions to stuff a dampened towel in the door gap.

Several spiders which had made their home unnoticed in the exhaust fan housing dropped down stone-cold dead. Doors slammed as my wife and children instantly became refugees, grabbed hats and coats and fled to seek breathable air elsewhere. I was abandoned and left alone to suffer my fate. The peculiar and noxious smell is putrid and penetrating. It is worse than burnt hair.

These disgusting 'alleged candies' are actually mislabeled 'prescription-only colonoscopy evacuation materials' only one of which is necessary to thoroughly empty any colon prior to scoping. I wouldn't wish these on my worst enemy.

Seriously, if you are scheduled for a colonoscopy, drop me a line and I will send you 20 of these nuclear option bowel evacuation 100% guaranteed to cleanse your bowels and make you wish for an end to life. Saves you money, no prescription needed.

Gummy Bears From Hell

Pain, flatulence, death

I knew what was coming the moment I swallowed one of these villainous bears. I had read the reviews, and I was prepared for the master cleanse. But I really couldn't prepare myself for the pain that was about to ensue. Nobody could possibly anticipate or fathom the hellish nightmare that is the sugar free deliciousness of Albanese Gummy Bears.

I received the 5 pound bag and immediately grabbed a handful of the little guys. Quite honestly, I thought I was immune to their powers because, after several hours, all I really experienced was some pretty foul flatulence. Then, I thought that I was hot shit and had FOUR more handfuls. I am not sure what I was thinking. After this, I laid down and began to fall asleep. It was about 9:30 in the evening.

And then it hit.

Noises. Oh my sweet Lord, the noises. It sounded like an old jalopy on its last hoorah. My family thought the dog was fighting with a cat and they were both were on the brink of death. Just truly awful sounds.

Round one hit like a freaking freight train. My feet actually were LIFTED off of the ground. I struggled to hold on. I've watched a lot of rodeos in my day, and the only thing I could think to do was grab onto the bottom of the toilet and ride that puppy out. I wish it was only an eight second ride. Round one was probably more like an eighteen-minute ride, but who really knows, because I lost all concept of time for the duration. It briefly slowed down, and thought for a fleeting moment, "Oh my lands, I think the horror is over."

How ignorant I was.

The next noise to come out of me can quite honestly only be describe as if someone stuck a leaf blower straight into a porcelain bowl filled with the blubber of a baby seal on full blast. The acoustics were incredible.

This noise was inevitably the start of what I only could assume to be rounds 2 through 7. For the next 6-8 hours, my body was ravaged, violated, and dare I say maliciously raped by these damn things. I passed food I had eaten as a small child, foods my mother had eaten while I was in the womb, and things my mother had eaten BEFORE she was pregnant with me. Literally anything you can think of. It just kept coming.

The worst part of the whole deal was that the gummies weren't chewed up like I assumed they would be, because I vividly remember thoroughly masticating the hell bears. These little jokers reincarnated themselves inside of me and plummeted towards my sphincter like a hundred paratroopers jumping right into the heart of the Vietcong. I feared for myself physically. I am not sure how long I sat in agony of the throne that I used to call my happy place. I will forever have Vietnam-level flashbacks anytime I look at the white porcelain. I will never be the same after this gummy bear cleanse.

I continued to camp out on the toilet until I mustered up the courage to crawl back to bed. However, when I attempted to stand, my legs buckled from weakness. I fell somehow under my sink. My face was buried in a mysterious pile of pubic hair and small, termite-like bugs. Still not sure what that was about. Nonetheless, I was thankful for the pubic pillow God had given me. It was far better than the burning pain of the gummy bears on my sphincters. I stayed in this same position for the rest of the day.

I am currently in physical recovery from this incident, although I will never recover completely mentally. This was a truly awful experience for both mind and body.

I gave his product 5 stars because it did exactly what it was supposed to do and more: the Gummy Bear Master Cleanse for $21. 10/10 would recommend to a friend.

Gummy Bears From Hell

The gastrointestinal pyrotechnics are 100% True.

I bought these with the intention of trying out a new snack to give my diabetic father-in-law. I read the reviews, and thought "oh silly internet with your trolling"...Boy was I wrong. To prove the haters wrong, I added in another piece of the challenge, the world's hottest chocolate bar.

So I invented a challenge called "Race to the finish." Basically, I ate one square of the chocolate a minute, and between squares, I pounded 10 of these delicious and soft, delectable, devil bears. It was not long after starting that I realized my mistake. I was tearing, drooling, sweating, and snotting. It was manageable, but the responses were uncontrollable, and that was just from the chocolate. Let me also say that the bears are deceivingly delicious and coax you to keep eating them with their adorable faces and delicious flavors.

Soon after the gurgling and churning began as the bears and chocolate went to war. It was World War 3 and the stage was my intestinal tract. I wish these bears were around when Hitler was a problem. Such a delicious innocent gift to cripple the Third Reich...I'm pretty sure MRE's I ate 15+ years ago in the Navy have been liquidated and expelled. I managed to make it through the entire chocolate bar, dipping the bears in it like Satan's fondue due to the weather making my chocolate bar a puddle.

I ate 60 bears total, and the aftermath was a tale for the ages. If you buy these bears, clear your schedule. My gut is iron, and this crippled me for 8 hours. I have read stories of people eating less, and being taken down for longer, days even. Don't be like me and buy these because you think everyone is lying...or a day later, you will be where I am right now, telling your tale of horror and regret in a product review.

No pants were soiled during the writing of this review, just a few close calls.

P.S. For the love of everything holy, it's not a fart. Don't trust it.

Everything they say is true....

So I've read the horror stories and it all sounded too good to be true. It wasn't. Everything that has been said in these reviews is 100% accurate. And so without further delay, here is my story...

I heard about these a long time ago and wanted to try them, but could never justify myself in spending $20 on an oversized pack of gummy bear disguised laxatives. However, I found a reason. I currently live with my family, including a younger brother of mine who likes to steal food and lie about it, thinking we'll never find out. Seriously, he'll take everything. One time he even stole an entire bulb of garlic and ate it in one sitting, then lied about it like we couldn't smell it. Don't worry, we feed him. He just has impulsive issues.

Anyways, I thought to myself, "Well shoot, if these gummies are what everyone says they are, time for a lesson he won't forget." And so with a click of the mouse and a doorbell ring later, they were sitting on my dresser waiting to be devoured.

I decided not to be too cruel and try them out myself. I wanted to be careful so I started with 5...nothing. Then 10...a couple rumbles but nothing serious. No trip to the bathroom yet. Then 15...one trip to the bathroom.

Then I got impatient.

About 6 hours ago I took two handfuls, counted them out (which ended up being 43 - more than doubling my previous dose) and ate them all within five to seven minutes. That was a poor choice.

I was sitting at the dinner table about an hour ago. Felt some rumbles and instantly knew, "The demon bears have arrived..." I was waiting for everyone to leave the table so I wouldn't look rude getting up first and as soon as I got up I felt some kind of gas leave me that I didn't even know existed. Also, I felt as something else might have left my body as well. I was in a panic. I instantly ran (or more like waddled) to the bathroom to assess the damage. Fortunately, it was just the gas the passed through and nothing else. I was relieved. But after another half hour they hit yet again, I knew better this time than to let anything escape so I ran to the restroom, quickly sat down, and let it rip.

Gummy Bears From Hell

Holy crap.

I had no idea I could put something solid in my mouth and it could come out as straight liquid on the way out. Like, I'm being serious. It was like a pressure washer spewing out of my butt. MULTIPLE TIMES. The smell, awful. The cramps, they make you want to die. I knew immediately that I was going to have a very, very long night.

Long story short, I chose to not give them to my brother. I don't want to go to jail for child abuse. However if you want a quick and tasty detox, these are definitely the trick.

Also, to those of you who think, "What a waste of time, he wrote a novel for a review." Yeah, well, I'm currently stuck on the toilet with nothing else better to do.

They really are delicious, but..........

Here I sit just melting away
The truth be told to you this day
Received as a gift from my bro I now hate
Heard the rumors, had to test my fate

So try these I did, just like a drone
Ate too many, now on the throne
Delicious and tasty I will admit
But the devil is inside each little bit

"What was I thinking?!!" I have to ask
Extinguishing the flames my only task
I pray to all in heaven so high
Make it stop before I die

3 hours on without any peace
What I would give to make this cease
The explosions that follow for all to hear
Will make one shudder and tremble in fear

I warn you this which comes from the heart
Caution after eating and don't trust a fart!!!

Gummy Bears From Hell

This one's for you, comrade

I originally bought these things with the intention of eating a few to see if anything happened. But after feeling no sudden effects for 2 hours, I decided they didn't work and gave some to the other tenents living here.

I said they could eat a many as they want but that's when I learned it was a bad idea. I was finally getting ready for bed when all of a sudden I felt the farts coming. I smiled and accepted this challenge thinking it would be no problem whatsoever. I went to sleep and woke up hours later in a pool of my own cold sweat and the sounds of what I can only describe as the gates of hell in my stomach.

I crawled to the bathroom and got on the toilet as fast and precise as possible, then I prepared for my bowels to erupt and quite possibly leave me dead.

It's currently 2 in the morning here where I'm at and I have been on the toilet for the last 20 mins erupting liquid fire out my ass. My roommate has been laughing his ass off the entire time while I sit and suffer on the toilet seat...

10/10 would buy these gummy bears again!

Slow painful death by Gummy Bears in an airplane bathroom

Ate a bag of these when I boarded a six-hour flight to Seattle.

Gastric explosion at 30,000 feet. Enough said.

My advice: don't use a bathroom on a Delta flight. That stench is from me...seven years ago.

These bears taste amazing, but(t).....

I read a lot of these reviews decided that they were a challenge, not a warning. I bought a 5 pound bag! The first night - Friday, just to make sure there were no accidents at work - I ate 20 of those delicious bears and waited about 30 minutes. I felt nothing!

I ate 10 more and waited 15 minutes. Still nothing! Finally, I manned up and ate 45 more. After I ate the last one, my stomach was warning me to stop. It felt like there were 2 giant bears fighting in my belly.

Finally, the gas started. I sat on the toilet, just in case one of those bears broke free! No accidents! I kept visiting the toilet until 1:30 AM. I think the bears got tired, as I did. No accidents throughout the night. I thought to myself, "I have conquered these vicious bears!"

The next day, I ate a handful or two. No problems. By Monday, I'm feeling very confident that I have an iron gut. I decided to show off to all the guys at work, and I didn't have one episode.

After work, I started my 25-minute trip home. That's when those evil bears woke up and started fighting in my belly! 10 minutes into my trip, I am handling it pretty well.

By minute 20, I'm sweating and clinching my bottom as tight as my sphincter would hold! I thought that I cut a button-hole in the seat with my butt!

25 minutes and I'm finally home! I run to my bathroom and stripped down to nothing. I wasn't sure what was about to happen! Before my butt hit the toilet seat, it starts! I think that I was having convulsions right up until the end! When I went to wipe with the standard White Cloud, it stuck there! I'm pretty sure that I was crapping pure gummy bears. I had to break out the flushable wipes. They were able to cut through the carnage!

By the time I got to the last wipe, I felt what I could only describe as a raisin shaped sore spot on the rim of my sphincter.

I go to the doctor tomorrow. I think that those evil bears caused such a violent bowel movement, that I might have developed a hemorrhoid! It's been there for over a week, and it's still sore to wipe with the standard TP. I had to buy a bulk size box of flushable wipes!

Gummy Bears From Hell

The legends are true

I was very curious about these bears after reading the reviews, so I bought a bag for my friend and I to eat and see if the rumors were true.

They were. We ate about 2 or 3 handfuls, and nothing happened for about an hour or so, but as we were on the sofa watching TV after some chicken and rice, I got real gassy. My friend waddled to the bathroom like a penguin and slammed the door behind him. About 30 seconds after he shut the door, I heard what sounded like an airplane running out of gas coming from my friend's bathroom. I then heard him yell that he pooped his pants.

Laughing, I fell on his sofa. Then he came out. About 30 minutes later, I felt it too. I rolled off my friend's sofa and crawled to the bathroom with my butt cheeks clenched tight. I sat on the toilet, and that's when I found out that I also pooped my pants. I proceeded to sit on the toilet for what felt like an eternity and my ass sounded like an elephant. After my friend threw my jeans and underwear in his washer, our stomachs cramped for the rest of the day and into the next day, but wore off after about 48 hours.

Our conclusion to this experiment is the rumors are true. Please eat responsibly or on an empty stomach

A most excellent prank

So here I was thinking it would be a good prank to put these out at a party in a bowl. About an hour into the party I noticed the little gummy bear shaped Ex-Lax were starting to go. As the host, I was all around the house and unable to keep an eye on the bowl of bears other than to keep it topped off. About an hour later, I was starting to think that they wouldn't have any affect.

It was right about then I realized the first victim was my sister as she sprung straight up off my couch with her legs locked out straight and she was unable to move. The noise from her stomach sounded like she was going to erupt as I giggled inside, thinking about how much she deserved it.

While she was in the bathroom, I noticed my aunt getting a little uncomfortable. She sat on my couch with her ass tightened up so much she had her legs crossed and they were straight out helping her keep her clench solid. She's now asking if anyone is in the bathroom. I had informed everyone my upstairs bathroom was broken so I could personally witness the destruction.

This went on and on, pushed their way through those two, a nephew, two nieces and my uncle. I was the only one that didn't eat them and they certainly didn't disappoint. It the total of three hours they were at my house they went through about 7 rolls of toilet paper. I can't wait to bring some to work!

Gummy Bears From Hell

Just don't. Unless it's a gift for someone you hate.

Oh man...words cannot express what happened to me after eating these. The Gummi Bear "Cleanse." If you are someone that can tolerate the sugar substitute, enjoy. If you are like the dozens of people that tried my order, RUN!

First of all, for taste I would rate these a 5. So good. Soft, true-to-taste fruit flavors like the sugar variety...I was a happy camper.

BUT (or should I say BUTT), not long after eating about 20 of these all hell broke loose. I had a gastrointestinal experience like nothing I've ever imagined. Cramps, sweating, bloating beyond my worst nightmare. I've had food poisoning from some bad shellfish and that was almost like a skip in the park compared to what was going on inside me.

Then came the, uh, flatulence. Heavens to Murgatroyd, the sounds, like trumpets calling the demons back to Hell...the stench, like 1,000 rotten corpses vomited. I couldn't stand to stay in one room for fear of succumbing to my own odors.

But wait; there's more. What came out of me felt like someone tried to funnel Niagara Falls through a coffee straw. I swear my sphincters were screaming. It felt like my delicate starfish was a gaping maw projectile vomiting a torrential flood of toxic waste. 100% liquid. Flammable liquid. NAPALM. It was actually a bit humorous (for a nanosecond) as it was just beyond anything I could imagine possible.

AND IT WENT ON FOR HOURS.

I felt violated when it was over, which I think might have been sometime in the early morning of the next day. There was stuff coming out of me that I ate at my wedding in 2005.

I had FIVE POUNDS of these innocent-looking delicious-tasting HELLBEARS so I told a friend about what happened to me, thinking it HAD to be some type of sensitivity I had to the sugar substitute, and in spite of my warnings and graphic descriptions, she decided to take her chances and take them off my hands.

Silly woman. All of the same for her, and a phone call from her while on the toilet (because you kinda end up living in the bathroom for a spell) telling me she really wished she would have listened. I think she was crying.

Her sister was skeptical and suspected that we were exaggerating. She took them to work, since there was still 99% of a 5 pound bag left. She works for a construction company, where there are builders, roofers, house painters, landscapers, etc. Lots of people who generally have limited access to toilets on a given day. I can't imagine where all of those poor men (and women) pooped that day. I keep envisioning men on roofs, crossing their legs and trying to decide if they can make it down the ladder, or if they should just jump.

If you order these, best of luck to you. And please, don't post a video review during the aftershocks.

PS: When I ordered these, the warnings and disclaimers and legalese were NOT posted. I'm not a moron. Also, not sure why so many people assume I'm a man. I am a woman. We poop, too. Of course, our poop sparkles and smells like a walk in a meadow of wildflowers. Thanks for all the great comments. I've been enjoying reading them and so glad that the horror show I experienced from snacking on these has at least made some people smile.

Gummy Bears From Hell

If you need some time off work these are for you

So there I was, innocently browsing Amazon for things I don't need, and I come across this product with the crazy reviews. I thought to myself, this is some massive joke! There is no way these can make you poop everywhere.

So after some deliberation I said "challenge accepted". When they arrived I ate a bunch, I was okay that time. So I assumed the reviews were wrong, and moved on with my life.

A few weeks later I'm craving a sweet snack and pull out the bag of bears. I ate until I couldn't anymore. Took a nap and woke up in the worst pain of my life! My belly was rumbling like I had swallowed a Tasmanian devil.

I get to the bathroom and let out the loudest, longest fart ever. My dog ran away in fear. I was then stuck of the toilet for what seemed to be an eternity. Luckily I had extra toilet paper. That was my only luck that day.

I questioned all my life choices that led to that moment and prayed to survive. Did not make it into work that day. The next day the gummy bears did make it into work. There the dietician ate too many and had to go home. I did not expect that as she spends her days telling patients what not to eat. But anyway, these may trick you into forgetting the first time you eat them, and then make you poop your pants. If you poop your pants at work you get the day off.

So is it worth it? You have to decide.

There will be blood

So I bought a 5 pound bag seeing if these little bastards held up to the sugar-free bears and boy...they did not disappoint.

Having 5 is the happy medium, you get to snack on some yummy treats without the worry of soiling yourself.

Anything over 5...you're on your own and may God be with you! Full Disclosure: I am writing this review on my toilet, where I have been off and on for the past 3 hours. Today at work, I decided that I would be a brave boy and push the limits of my body. So I ate roughly 25-30 of these cyanide pills.

Two hours later: What I can only describe as someone with a voodoo doll twisting me in half, hits me. "Ok boys, I'm headed home" I shout to my coworkers. I make it to my truck as the cramping intensifies. "Manageable" I say to myself, "I can surely make the 15-minute trip home." Approximately 30 seconds later, I am sitting inside of a plastic shopping bag, completely convinced that I will not make it home.

I MADE IT!!! I gingerly walk into my home and up the stairs, all the while the sounds of a horribly executed exorcism are playing out in my twisted-up gut. The second that I touch porcelain what can only be compared to dropping a Mentos into a 2 liter of Diet Coke followed. Unfortunately, this was just the beginning. Over the past 3 hours, the eruptions have been coming at a steady pace. My toilet/ass must be feeling what the Allied forces felt like against the German Blitzkrieg.

The horrendous sound of demons screaming in your gut, is like an alarm clock without the snooze button. Do not lollygag when you hear them chant, you just run. And this should go without saying, under NO CIRCUMSTANCES trust a fart! I cannot stress that last part enough. I hope that you heed my warnings and prepare properly. Treat this as if it were a blizzard and stock up on just TP, forget the milk unless you are lactose intolerant and want the ultimate flush.

All in all I give this product 5/5 stars and would recommend this to a friend. I am currently placing an order for another 5lb bag...

Gummy Bears From Hell

Explosion from the anus

Definitely lived up to the expectations. Ate almost half the bag in one day and spent the next 3 regretting everything life decision I ever made.

Ran all my loved ones away. Made the dog vomit due to the disgusting smells and sounds that were coming from my anus. Screw buying over-the-counter laxatives. Eat 3-4 handfuls of these gummies and they will clear every bit of food inside your stomach out. Had me honestly thinking I was on my death bed.

Due to the current covid situation I thought something was seriously wrong. But I'd buy them again in a heartbeat.

Butt nuclear missile

Five stars if your goal was to murder your insides.

I ordered these gummy bears as a prank on my friends. So the package came and I took them to my school and started handing them out, I offered 25 to my friend and ate 3 to make it not seem suspicious.

Well, those three bears started churning my insides and I can only describe it as if you are on a roller coaster and your stomach drops.

My friend ate two handfuls, and I warned him about what was to come, 1 hour and 17 mins later he's on the toilet. He described it as if someone had attached a hose to his anus and turned it on full blast. Chunks of black liquid feces poured out of his anus for 3 hours straight - he ate the gummy bears about 4 hours ago and has been to the bathroom 10 times so far.

That's not even the worse part. These bears also like to come out of your mouth to these little bears made a geyser in my stomach and shot out like a fire hose on a building. I could have used my vomit projectiles as a nuke on ISIS. It happened to my other friends to. Buy these at your own risk

Oh My God!

These are the most delicious sugar-free candies I have ever tasted. The wife and I ordered them and we were so excited when they arrived. She was home and I actually drove home from work on my lunch break to sample them. Oh my God! They are so delicious. We ate a couple of handfuls. We were so happy with them that we let the kids eat them too. All that evening, we were indulging in these delicious little bears.

But then it happened...

It started with a little rumble in the top left part of the abdomen. Then it became a gurgle in the lower right. After a little while, what I thought was going to be a simple bout of flatulence took an immediate turn for the worst. The sound that escaped from me led me to believe that what had escaped my rear end was not only air, but also a bit of liquid. I hurried to take care of that.

Later that night, while in bed, the worst happened. These delicious bears brought destruction to my rectum unlike anything I've experienced in my 48 years of life. Thinking I had gas...no...not gas...projectile poops! Bed, floor, toilet, ceiling, it was like something out of a Freddy Kruger movie!

These bears are DELICIOUS! But just know that you will ruin your streak of not pooping on yourself, your things, and on others! These things give you the worst diarrhea you will EVER experience in your life! But they're delicious.

Gummy Bears From Hell

Curiosity very nearly killed the cat

Alright, here's my review: I bought these because of all the comments that claimed they would cause diarrhea and/or massive gas, etc., had made me curious. Heck, I'm curious like a cat; that's why my friends call me 'Whiskers'.

Anyways, I don't care for sugar-free anything, am not afraid of getting diarrhea (I'm usually constipated anyways) and have always been amused with having excess flatulence.

So, to start with...the taste. I think the taste of anything and everything 'sugar free' kind of sucks no matter what but I must admit, these actually weren't that bad. The pineapple ones were the best, I thought, and the lemon ones were my least favorite. I only noticed an aftertaste from the aspartame after I stopped eating them and even then, it wasn't as bad as from a diet soda or what not. I started off eating about 20 of them.

I had a normal bowel movement about 2 hours later, nothing out of the ordinary. About 2 hours after that, it was Mount St. Colons for about 10 minutes. Afterwards, I had some pretty rancid gas that seemed to last about 3 hours. Conclusion: potent as advertised. On a side note, I gave some to one of my coworkers (he had about 15 or so) and he told me about 2 hours later, he was on the thundermug blasting out a rooster tail.

Since I'm lactose intolerant, I think I'll have some of these with a glass of milk. I should be weaponized pretty good.

Epic farewell!

I wanted devil bears to take to my last day of work and torture my co-workers. I did some research and discovered these had the spawn of Satan ingredient in them, so off to work I went with these little demons. I was filled with excitement and fear the entire drive in. Not to mention filled with gas from the Bears I stupidly ate the night before. Fat kid problems.

Fast forward to everyone showing up in the office (supervisors excluded - making it an epic last day). We reluctantly started eating these delicious bastards, some not convinced they would have any reaction to it. Fast forward about an hour, and contestant number one made a mad dash to the bathroom, not to be seen again for a while.

Return from the bathroom, and said co-worker appears flushed (no pun intended). 15 minutes later.... spawn of Satan returned to take the same co-worker's rectum hostage. The rest of us stopped eating at the first signs of the co-worker's colon death sprint.

I wish I could say we were saved from the carnage, but I would be lying. The sounds coming from our guts sounded like angry whales and the cramps were worse than I could have imagined. Our eyes popped out of our heads with every violent growl of our intestines, yet we were unable to contain our laughter. One co-worker went from laughing and joking to silent and a total look of fear. He zoned out from our discussions, looked dazed, and panic set in on his now pale face. It became apparent. The guy who can't drop a deuce in public is now focusing all his energy on NOT dropping a dose of hot bear lava his pants! Haha. It was an amazingly noisy and smelly day as farts flew, and the fear of sharting our pants grew stronger and stronger every minute. These little bastard bears were worth every penny!

Gummy Bears From Hell

Let me tell you a story...

...a story of four innocent teenagers going about their day at high school when things took a turn for the worse.

It all started early in the morning, out in the parking lot, when I took the bag out of my backpack, offering it to my friends. Every one of them ate several handfuls of these delicious little things. Little did they know these gummy bears started wreaking havoc on their digestive track the moment they entered it; and wreak havoc they did.

It was first hour, and I could already hear my friend's stomach crying for help, but being the shy kid he is, he tried waiting it out. It did not abate, but he held out till the end of class. He was slow to get up and out of his desk, raising himself mostly with his arms for he was afraid to let slip the tides of hell. Knees-crossed, he slowly waddled over to the bathroom to wage war on a poor, unsuspecting toilet. I feel bad for that toilet, it could have been having a good day until my friend walked in. Like a casualty of war, I had to leave my friend to fight his battles alone.

As I walked to my next class I heard rumors, whispers of a kid who let a fart loose; nearly s***ting himself he had to leave class for the bathroom, and no one saw him since. I immediately knew it was another friend of mine, another casualty.

It was here that I asked myself, "Should I have warned them?" But I quickly pushed the thought aside, for this day was one of the funniest I've had the privilege of witnessing and my plan was working without a hitch.

Lunch time, I was looking forward to regrouping with all my friends, to see who was left and who had fallen victim to these hell bears. Only one had shown up, I couldn't stop the grin that slowly appeared across my face. But that grin was dwarfed by the laugh I gave after lunch. The one friend that survived only survived because he had nothing in his system, like an unloaded gun. But once that gun was loaded, that gun fired...and fired...and fired.

All four fell victim, all four essential players in the school's football team, all four missing from the game that night. Me and my real group of friends laughed and reminisced as we watched our team loose. We laughed because I had made a nice sized bet as to which team would win. These gummy bears literally made me money, and that's worth five stars.

Wow!

This demon candy will force its way through your GI tract lickity-split. After eating maybe ten of these innocent looking delicious hell bears, I noticed that there started a grumbling from my insides. Before I knew it, I was involuntarily squeezing my sphincter shut to hold back the devilish tide of lava juice that was trying to force its way out. Good luck and may God have mercy on all who dare to partake in this sacrament.

Gummy Bears From Hell

Sharing is caring

I bought these at a local convenience store before I went to work thinking nothing could go wrong.

I brought them in for a meeting so my coworkers could share during the meeting. My boss was the first one to take a handful and eat in one sitting when I just got to work. 10 mins later I put them in a plastic bowl so everyone could snack, 20 mins later the meeting begins and discuss the margins of our service performance.

While one of our co-workers was pointing something out about a customer service, I heard a growl coming from boss's chair. For a second, I thought he had an angry Pitbull right beside him but then I saw his face turn red and he groaned a little. I thought he was feeling a bloated from something he ate and then two other employees started sweating a little. I ate for of those demon bears and I too started to feel the spell. We still had another 2 hours into the meeting and everyone looked like they were starting to get ill, but we still pushed on without anyone saying a word and trying to act normal.

One of the employees stumbles out of the meeting room and we hear this enormous thunderous blast echo down the hallway sounding like an artillery piece going off in a building. Then another employee face turns red and passes out, face-planting into the meeting table and sharts explosively causing him to eject out of the seat onto the floor.

This is just the beginning. Everyone in the room ran out of the meeting room like it was life or death and that a causes a chain reaction of sharting left and right. we only had many stalls for those poor unfortunate souls. My boss got the worst of it when he was trying walk down the hallway a loud explosive fart would follow each and every step along with a few others.

By the time I got out to the hallway, it was already covered in liquid bears and people were pushing each other to get it the restrooms, I remember this one poor petite lady was propelled down the hallway by this phenomenon.

It was every man for himself, people were fighting over stalls and even trash cans, by the end of the day hazmat team had to come in and clean up this horrific mess, worst day at work ever

POOnami

What fresh hell is this?

I bought them as a joke, but an hour after eating far too many of them I broke out in a fever.

20 minutes after that, my stomach felt like someone was playing trampoline basketball and running towards my colon. I barely sat down in time before the first tsunami of poo broke the bottom of the bowl.

I'm pretty sure the fire alarm going off right now here at work, is my fault. But I can't evacuate the building, until I finish evacuating my bowels.

The first responder beating on the door asking "Is everything alright in there??"

Seriously dude? Obviously not.

The POOnami is the reason the fire alarm is ringing.
If I COULD leave I would. But I can't.

Oh...and send the plumber this way, if you get a chance.

Gummy Bears From Hell

The Legend is true!

I was skeptical of the other reviews and thought most of this was just fun by a softy who can't handle a little gas. Wrong.

Package arrived approximately 5pm. I had a small bag of them by 7pm. Now it's a little after midnight and I am laughing at my wife (who I woke from a dead sleep) carrying burning candles into the bathroom and doing some Catholic prayer for me.

To be very clear: if you want to play games with these gummy bears, make sure you bring a Bluetooth speaker into the bathroom and play some music on at least 80 percent max or everyone in the house is gonna know what you are doing in there.

Truly, I eat spicy and ethnic foods frequently. Just one pack of these gummy bears have made a mess of my insides. They were delicious and pretty low calorie but you have been warned.

Great taste, violent aftermath

These gummies work well as a laxative. They only take an hour to kick in and your colon will spend the next four hours cleansing itself at your sphincter's expense. I suggest coupling your purchase with some cooling wet wipes beforehand.

I have seen the face of God

I didn't feel the need to plan my weekend around five small gummy bears. But if you fail to plan, you plan to fail.

It began with a noticeable change in the viscosity of my saliva. Within minutes of consumption, my mouth had filled with a thick foamy slime. Though I was in a cool climate-controlled room, a salty sweat broke out. I felt my heartbeat quicken as my body threw itself into fight or flight mode.

The animal noises broadcasting from my pelvis were an ominous warning of the violent acts that were to follow. I shouldered my way into the bathroom, clawing at my belt, moaning with pain. The smell came first. It started sweet, almost tangy. That was quickly overpowered by a cloying chemical perfume.

The first volley of feces hit the water like soda cans and nickels. The resulting splash drenching my bottom in foul brackish water, but this quickly became the least of my worries.

After another moment, the noises in my core hit a fever pitch and I was struck rigid with pain. The sweat was now running into my eyes, but the room had turned ice cold and my hands began to spasm.

I felt an insidious burning flooding my escape hatch. I gasped. Hot yellow poison began spraying from my rear, changing in pitch and echo as the stream of diarrhea whipped around the toilet bowl, creating a nightmarish Doppler effect that can only be appreciated in hindsight. My legs fell asleep sitting on the toilet. I couldn't have stood up if I wanted to.

Wiping was a no-go. Toilet paper simply became a vile paper mache'. My hands were quickly soiled. A full-blown shower was needed, and all of my towels had to be burned.

So happy with my purchase, would recommend to friends and definitely buying again!

Gummy Bears From Hell

Could be used to torture information from terrorists.

It was my first deployment and I had been missing a lot of stuff from the states. I could get gummy bears at the PX here but not the sugar-free ones, and with the army weight regulations I try to keep my snacking healthy. Thus, when I saw a 5 pound bag of sugar-free gummies I couldn't help but put the order in.

The gummies shipped in a verily fast manner and I was relieved to notice that none of the gummies appeared to have melted or been damaged in any way. When I got the bag, I was somewhat shocked, seeing for the first time how much 5 pounds of gummy bears actually is. I knew there would be no way for me to consume them all myself. Luckily, we had a range later that week. I stashed the gummies in my wall locker until the range.

On range day, we all sat under some camo nets we had put up to protect us from the sun as we waited our turn to qualify. During this time, I broke out the gummies. Everyone was stoked. We all sat around chatting as we ate delicious soft squishy gummies washed down with Rawdatain water. So far, the range had been going smoothly. Soon it was my turn to fire. I was given range 3 and I immediately got into pronc as this range starts off from the prone supported position. I adjusted my sand bags and that's when I realized something wasn't right.

It start with just a gurgle and then a grimacing pain. I could hear the range control over the loudspeaker "Firers, prepare to fire. Lock and load your weapons" GURGLE- the noise was terrible and the pain was horrific. I tried to focus on the target by my vision started to blur and sweat poured into my shooting eye.

All the while, "Firers, place your selector switch from safe to semi." I could no longer feel my hands they had gone numb. I realized at that moment I had to go and I mean GO.

And then it came: "Firers, at this time you may fire your weapons." I didn't move my switch from safety; even if my hands weren't numb, I wouldn't have trusted myself with a loaded weapon. Now, I had another problem. The range was hot! I heard firing around all around me. I weakly fumbled with my weapon and placed it in a safe position.

The Range Safety came up to me. "Soldier, is there something wrong?" The look I gave must have gave said it all. The safety waved his paddle and the call was made. "Cease fire! Cease fire! Cease FIRE!"

I was up and looking for relief. While the other soldiers had stopped firing, my colon had just begun. I made a rush to the porta johns to find they were all filled up. Of course. I had shared those gummies with at least 10 other troops. The noises coming out of those porta pots will cause PTSD for many years to come. I thought for a second about finding a place out of sight. However, it was futile, I was in the desert you could see for miles all around. Then I remember the Nationals had a porta pot and likely no one else knew it was there. It was under the range control tower surrounded by a small fence.

I rushed, as quickly as possible in my condition, clenching my cheeks and praying to every god I had ever heard of. I made it and found it was unoccupied. I opened the door to find, in my dismay, an eastern toilet.

I began to take all my gear off in a hurry. All the while, small amounts of air slipped past my cheeks with a liquid-like feel. "Oh gods!" I thought. I clenched tighter ripping my boots off I could tell I would need all my clothing off as this was likely to cause to cause an immense backsplash.

Finally, disrobed, I allowed the release....it was a clumpy tidal wave of destruction. The smell was nothing of this world. I tried not to vomit as my anus took on a will of its own, expelling this sickness from my system.

After finishing, I looked down in horror at the Eastern Toilet realizing there was no way that this was going to drain properly. I accepted defeat at my attempt to clean up the terrible smelly gummy soil and washed myself up with some baby wipes I so mercifully had in my ACU pocket.

I put my clothes on and stumbled out of the toilet. As I walked, one of the natives walked by me. I tried to warn him, but he didn't understand. I only heard him cry out "Allah" as he slammed the door walking away from the porta pot looking at me with fear, the eyes

Gummy Bears From Hell

telling it all. He couldn't understand how that could have come out of a human being without killing them.

In the end, 10 troops were given saline solution for dehydration from the terrible gummies. Our unit swore a vow of secrecy to never speak of this experience again with one another because of the back flashes that some still have.

Gummy From Hell

I live in what used to be Tucson, Arizona, and after this story is done you will know why I say used to be. I am 34 years old and work as a contractor. I'm a bit of a health nerd who works out seven times a week and eats only the top-of-the-line protein shakes and other nastiness that is my lifes blood. I'm single, and after this I doubt any lady will ever come near me again.

Anyways, one day in my normal everyday life I decide to peruse the internet and to a lesser extent online shopping systems. My teeth were unfortunate enough to have a sweet tooth and nothing in my kitchen was anywhere near sugar-free yet sweet to the core, so I decided that I may as well search for something that might satisfy me in times like this.

Then the miracle that is Gummy Bears came upon my search window. The price for a 5-pound bag was nothing if not a steal, so my finger decided to hover over the purchase button, and for a moment my finger just stood there a ominous sign for the things to come. With overzealous enthusiasm I pressed the order button and thus my death was secured.

A week and a half later after much anticipation my bears arrived at the door. I was surprised that when I opened the box that none of the bears had melted in the hot sweltering heat that is Arizona, a foreshadowing for just how indestructible this substance is.

I was overjoyed and after the week and a half of saving myself for these delicate gummy snacks, I decided I may as well use that day as my cheat day.

I sat on my couch with the bag in my lap and turned on House. Luckily for me I had the entire series on DVR and, as it was a Saturday, I had no obligations other than to sit and eat my new snack.

Four hours later and 124 gummies later, Dr Cuddi (sp?) had finally fired the damn son of a b*&ch. My life was good at this moment - I was chewing on a gummy bear, my sweet tooth was satisfied, and I was in complete bliss.

Gummy Bears From Hell

As I continued to the next episode, my gut was extended to the point that I realized it was time to stop. Unfortunately it was already too late - the damage had already been done to my digestive tract.

A moment later the first of many gastrointestinal shudders started. My stomach started off l at a low rumble, and proceeded to a loud roar of a jet engine taking off for the last time.

My bowels were about to explode at this point and I felt substance leaking out. Needless to say, I chose to attempt to make my way to the restroom across the hall, waddling like a penguin to the safety of my ivory bowl.

Unlucky for me, though, my restroom is over 15 feet across my house and I was nowhere near able to hold myself for that long a trek.

It was at this moment against the excruciating pain that I thought back to that moment when my finger hovered over the 'buy' button on that fateful night, and looked back at it in a third person view wishing to be able to yell to myself that the button should never be pressed. I sat in horror as I watched the button pressed and was instantaneously returned back to the hallway where my colon was excreting mass liters of substance and I was in desperate need of a john.

Pulling myself up, I forced my way to the throne that is my toilet and didn't even bother to close the door. As my rear end met the cool plastic my rectum could no longer hold the flow of old faithful (which now looking back was nowhere near the pressure that was exerted from my intestines). Hot molten fire was pushed through me and to the point where my toilet bowl was near past its breaking point.

It was at this moment good Saint Paul that I came to these Pearly Gates. The monument that is this angel turned to me and pinched his nose. The smell of my restroom had found its way past the ground zero that is Tucsan and had risen to the clouds of heaven.

The face Saint Paul made was one of disgust and pure terror. An instant later I was kicked down from cloud nine and sent hurtling to my body down below.

Thanks to Gummy Bears, I know am a godly man, I have given up the life of a fitness freak and now live as a monk off in the Sierra, Nevada, away from any who may still smell the stench.

Gummy Bears From Hell

The "wetting" of my pants

Dear Lord. I feel as though these gummies are the things that have made me get a colostomy about two years ago.

In May, 2012, I had a wedding to attend. Little did I know that they stocked sugar-free gummy bears as snacks at the hotel. Knowing myself, I had to down a couple before going to my cousin's wedding.

Once we finally got to the wedding Chapel, I noticed that something felt odd. It wasn't a cramp, it wasn't a stomach ache, but a mix of the two. I brushed it off after a while, but it soon got worse. Little did I know that what these little pains were inside of me turning out to be huge clumps of nuclear human waste.

Since I was the best man, I had to stand next to my cousin. This is only the icing on the cake. The stomach ache had gotten so bad, I had to let out a small fart. Bad decision. I immediately felt a warm liquid drip down my leg and onto the white carpet. Luckily, I was wearing slacks so nobody noticed.

I then decided to let out another one, but this time it was a sound of great magnitude. You could probably have heard this explosion of my anus from the very back of the chapel. All eyes were immediately on me. I ran out of the chapel as fast as my diarrhea-filled pants would let me run.

Soon, my brother came after me asking what was wrong. I ran into some nearby bushes to eradicate the rest of my vile waste that has churned into soapy, liquidy, explosive diarrhea. This time, there were some kids playing soccer out in a small clearing by some trees. Their eyes were on me, too. I again was forced to run away with my soiled slacks dragging against the road leaving behind a bloody trail.

After I found a new set of bushes by a local park which was thankfully empty, I continued the emptying of my bowels.

After about two hours of non-stop explosion of diarrhea from my anus, I had to call my brother. He ran over to the park, which was clearly visible from the chapel, and he noticed my condition. He called 911 upon noticing my bloody feces and an ambulance soon came. After a week in the hospital, I was ready for my surgery. I needed a colostomy due to my rectum being absolutely destroyed from the pressure in which the diarrhea came out. Now I have to carry a disgusting colostomy bag to poop in through my stomach.

Thanks a lot you idiots at the manufacturer who are probably laughing their asses off reading these reviews. I will however give this a two star because they did taste very good.

Don't mix baseball and these devils

I first had these gummies when I was about to play a kid-pitch game for my baseball league when I was about nine. I remember going to a birthday party earlier that day in which we went inside a candy shop and were allowed to get a half-pound of whatever candy we wanted.

So I choose to get these sugar-free gummy bears because gummy bears were my favorite snack and I had never ever had the sugar-free kind before. So, on the way over to my baseball game, I decided to have a couple to give me some energy. I remember getting to the field and doing some sliding drills before the game.

Next thing you know, I am sliding into second and felt something weird, but just played it cool. Next thing you know, my intestines felt like they caught fire and I couldn't stop sharting (I learned what the word meant that day). It was the worst experience ever.

I was sitting in the stall of the bathroom, farting and sharting for like 30 consecutive seconds at a time. I didn't know what was going on, I was having to flush about 3 times. I ended up missing a couple innings of my game, but I learned a valuable lesson, and where the term "when you are sliding into first and you feel a wet burst, diphtheria" originated.

Only use these if you need to get out of something quickly. They are the best form of laxatives on the market. Also, they are the perfect gift to give to someone you don't like, or to disguise as vodka gummy bears to get the frat guys to have a night to remember. Best form of laxatives on the market and, hey, you don't have to disguise it either.

Gummy Bears From Hell

Hurts so good!

I am truly at a loss for words on where to begin. On a whim about a month and a half ago, I purchased my first 5 lb bag of Haribo Gummi Bears. It arrived in 2 days and was packaged quite nicely. When I opened the box and saw the size of the bag I thought "Hmmm. That's a lot of gummi." I set it in my kitchen and forgot about them the first night.

When I woke up the next morning and was getting ready to leave for work, I decided I would open them and take a handful with me out the door. 7:30am is kind of an odd time to enjoy gummies I know, but they were there and I figured what the heck.

That moment single-handedly changed my life. I can't decide if it was for the better or for the worse. As soon as I popped a couple gummies into my mouth, it was like I transcended from my body and was looking down at myself. It was literally a flavor explosion and I was at ground zero!

I ended up not going to work that day in order to finish off the entire bag. Did I get sick? You bet. Three times. I found myself vomiting from the sheer amount of sweetness and the expansion of my stomach. As soon as I finished vomiting I went back to the bag for more!

Since that day I have purchased an additional bag of Gummi bears. I find myself separating them by color so I can decide what flavor to get sick on next. I have managed to get back to work, albeit totally distracted. All I find myself doing is sitting in my office, dreaming about getting home and getting sick of Haribo Gummis. This is the closest thing to heaven I have ever experienced.

Don't buy just because it's in a nice box

Oh man...words cannot express what happened to me after eating these. The Gummi Bear "Cleanse". If you are someone that can tolerate the sugar substitute, enjoy. If you are like the dozens of people that tried my order, RUN!

For taste I would rate these a 5. So good. Soft, true-to-taste fruit flavors like the sugar variety.

BUT (or should I say BUTT), not long after eating about 20 of these all hell broke loose. I had a gastrointestinal experience like nothing I've ever imagined. Cramps, sweating, bloating beyond my worst nightmare. I've had food poisoning from some bad shellfish and that was almost like a skip in the park compared to what was going on inside me.

Then came the, uh, flatulence. Heavens to Murgatroyd, the sounds, like trumpets calling the demons back to Hell...the stench, like 1,000 rotten corpses vomited. I couldn't stand to stay in one room for fear of succumbing to my own odors.

But wait; there's more. What came out of me felt like someone tried to funnel Niagara Falls through a coffee straw. I swear my sphincters were screaming. It felt like my delicate starfish was a gaping maw projectile vomiting a torrential flood of toxic waste. 100% liquid. Flammable liquid. NAPALM. It was actually a bit humorous (for a nanosecond)as it was just beyond anything I could imagine possible.

AND IT WENT ON FOR HOURS.

I felt violated when it was over, which I think might have been sometime in the early morning of the next day. There was stuff coming out of me that I ate at my wedding in 2005

Gummy Bears From Hell

Husband says they're great for weight control

Bought these having already read the reviews and let them sit on our counter until my husband (who has a sweet tooth) dipped into the bag and proceeded to eat about 40 of them.

About half an hour later he commented that he was going to use the bathroom and I tried my best to keep a straight face. He came back into the room about 15 minutes later complaining that he suddenly had "mud butt." I said nothing.

A few minutes after that he got up and went to the bathroom again. This time I could not contain my laughter and confessed what I had done. He laughed about it, luckily.

Altogether, he ended up having diarrhea for about 36 hours. Seriously, a day and a half of pooping every 45 minutes or so. These are amazing. 1,000 stars.

It's coming out of me like lava!

I now truly understand what she was talking about in Bridesmaids when she said, "It's coming out of me like lava!"

Not only is it liquid, pure liquid like throwing up from my butt, but it was also the loudest thunder farts I've ever had. Not to mention my stomach sounds like two bobcats are in there fighting.

Poo-Poo-Kachoo: my diarrhea-inducing journey

I'm like a lot of other people. I've read the reviews for the Sugar-Free Gummy Bears and laughed my hiney off. For me, though, that wasn't enough. I wanted to willingly subject myself to the hell bears of lore.

The unfortunate catch is that the five-pound bag of actual name brand candies is $136. I'm in college. Ain't nobody got money for that. So, with Google as my trusted companion, I went digging to see exactly what in the sugar-free bears caused people such volatile, poo-related escapades.

I quickly found the culprit to be a chemical compound known as lycasin. Now lycasin has a fun little ingredient in it called maltitol. This, ladies and gentleman, is your diarrhea-inducing little devil of a sugar substitute. So I thought to myself, "Why not search Amazon for lycasin?" Lo and behold, after a quick search, this very product popped up. Reading through a few of the other reviews assured me that this was what I was looking for, and for quite a paltry sum at that.

So, armed with my free trial of an online buying service, I placed my order. Fast forward two days later (yesterday). True to their word, my gummy tummy moshers arrived. Upon opening the packaging, I happened to glance over the ingredient list on the front of the product. The first one listed? Maltitol. That's a bingo.

I would have launched my fearless march into the realm of explosive bowel movements right then had I not already made plans to meet a friend for drinks that night. Two beers, one shot of whiskey, and several hours later I'm back home with my sweet gummy atrocities watching 30 Rock with my roommates. In one sitting, I took out half of the one-pound bag.

Is that an irresponsible, stupid decision? You bet your bottom dollar it is. Do I really give two shakes? No, sir/ma'am. Being an American, college-age male, it is my inalienable right to lurch from one poor decision to the next until I'm finally forced to start my life. However, that is somewhat beside the point.

After ingesting a half-pound of the delicious-tasting gummies, I passed out on the couch at a little past midnight. Now fast forward again to four hours later. I'm awakened by mild bloating and

Gummy Bears From Hell

moderate abdominal pain. Knowing what awaits, I shuffle to the upstairs bathroom and sit myself down upon the throne.

What happened next can only be accurately described by the words "butt vomit." A predominantly liquid composition, lightly flecked with solid matter shot from my bum-hole with all the force of a thousand suns. This continued for a half-hour as my body continued to forcibly banish all non-essential liquids to the porcelain bowl. Finally, I felt confident enough to clean myself up and go back to sleep.

Again at seven, the same gut-pain and rumblies in my tummy urged me to seek refuge atop my porcelain tower. In much the same fashion, watery waste material was banished from my colon in a flourish of squelching flatulence and churning of bowels. And again in a half hour, my second tour of duty (or rather "doody") was at an end.

However, in comparison to many of the other reviews posted about these types of candies, I can honestly say that it was not white-hot magma shooting out of my poop cannon, nor was it accompanied by the vile smells of high-decibel farts. Farts? Yes. Copious butt-vomit? You bet. Torturous experience? Not on any level. It is now eight and a half hours after eating the stanky bears that I'm composing this review. Have the effects entirely subsided? Not at all. I expect my stomach to hate me for at least a few more hours before normalcy returns to my bowels. It did give me a very ample excuse for not attending class this morning though.

As for the product itself, it absolutely delivered in every way I expected it to. The bears themselves are delightfully tasty, which only seems to be a guise for their malicious intent of liquefying the contents of your stomach and forcing them through your sphincter faster than a stampeding herd of cattle. For any intrepid traveler wishing to embark on a delectable, yet liquid-poo-inducing voyage, these bears are the way to do it on a budget. If you do decide to take that fateful leap, may you remember the words of David Bowie: "Check ignition, and may God's love be with you."

Doctors Orders

One of our beloved physicians brought a bag of gummy bears to work to share with the staff one night shift. Not realizing they were the famous dreaded sugar-free gummies, multiple staff throughout the shift grabbed a handful of gummies while passing by and each have their own near-miss stories. This is mine...

The next morning I have to run an errand about an hour and a half from my house. On the drive home down a curvy back country road my stomach suddenly begins to cramp and I feel the immediate urge to empty my bowels.

Frantic, as I realize I'm not going to make it home, I start searching for a place to pull over. The end of a gated logging road perhaps?

I'm speeding along, arching my back, practicing lamas breathing techniques, anything to stall the inevitable. I pass the first turnoff that has a Sheriff's car parked at the end and keep searching with sweat pouring down my forehead and bubbling noises in my guts that drown out the heavy metal on the stereo.

Finally! I spot the end of a brushy trail and whip my truck sideways, thrusting the driver's side door open and leaping from the seat to scurry around to the other side. I turn around with fingers in waste band about to drop trow and look up to my horror realizing it is indeed the end of a driveway and the folks outside are staring down toward me probably wondering what this crazed individual is about to do. For several moments, I seriously considered just completing the task and running away but couldn't imagine my parents seeing the cell phone video of myself on social media later in the day.

I scurried back around the truck and halfway there my ability to hold back the hot lava flow of liquid stool from making a hasty exit out of my spasming rectum was lost and I crapped my pants right there on the side of the road standing next to my truck. My bowels cramped up and expelled every drop of liquid from my body.

At that point I'm now standing there with leggings full of hot liquid stool running into my shoes and debating on what the next best course of action should be. Of course I have no extra clothes or any

Gummy Bears From Hell

towels in my truck. What do I do? Do I call someone? Do I drive home the remaining 20 minutes?

After a few moments of self-reflection, I decided to strip off my shirts and lay them on the seat of my truck and get inside. It was a rather uncomfortable drive home with the windows all down and skin burning on the backs of my legs and buttocks. It was one of the longest 20-minute periods of time I've ever experienced in my entire life.

I alternated between crying and laughing at the situation and checking the speedometer like a paranoid drunk thinking I can't possibly get pulled over right now because what would I say? Yes officer, I crapped my pants. That's what that smell is. Tears streaming down my face, I finally arrive home, screeching to a halt in the driveway in front of the open automatic garage door I triggered as I was drifting the curve onto my road. Holding the bottoms of my pant legs closed tight I awkwardly stagger into my house and immediately into the shower fully clothed.

Fast forward 3 weeks and I'm at work hearing about the other incidents and the light bulb clicks on……

35 years old and I had to reset the clock for the "how long since you've last crapped your pants" countdown….

Thanks Dr Hanson. Lesson learned…….make sure the gummy bears are not the sugar-free version

One of the worst days of my life

I ate half of a 6-ounce bag I picked up at a CVS. They changed the color of the bag. I didn't know. I spent 24 hours in the fetal position on the bathroom floor repeating "Please God, why?" I still don't have an answer.

This is your Captain speaking: Do not eat the red Gummy Bear. You'll be sorry.

Before a company goes public, the high-level executives embark on a multi-city tour with their investment bankers to drum up support for the upcoming IPO. This trip is called a roadshow and since the group will typically visit dozens of cities on a tight schedule, a private jet is the preferred means of transportation. During a roadshow, it's not unusual to visit two or three cities in a single day so work starts at the crack of dawn. But that doesn't mean the group goes to bed early. Every night, the bankers treat their clients to a wild night, complete with complimentary Gummy Bears and coffee. No matter how hard the group parties the night before, the private jet will lift them off to their next destination very early the next morning.

Just for a minute, pretend you're an investment banker traveling with some very important clients on one of these roadshows. Now imagine that you spent the previous night "dropping Yogi" way beyond your limit only to be startled out of bed by a piercing 6:30 am wake up call. In an attempt to get your head and body feeling remotely human again, you scarf down some more warm Gummy Bears and at least two glasses of coffee at the hotel's breakfast buffet before jumping on the shuttle to the private airport. Within a few minutes of arriving at the airport, your entire group is seated and the plane begins to taxi down the runway. At this point you might feel a bit of relief as the morning's blur subsides. All you have to do is sit back and relax for the one-hour flight to the next city.

There's just one problem. In your rush to get out of the hotel, down to breakfast and onto the plane you forgot to do one very crucial thing. Go to the bathroom. And I'm not talking about peeing. You have a stomach full of last nights multi-colored death bears and coffee churning around your lower intestine at 30,000 feet. But that's not the worst part. True horror sets in when you realize you're not on a spacious 20 person G5 with couches, beds, lay-z boys and a fully tucked away private bathroom. No, on this day you are traveling on a six-person puddle jumper sitting shoulder to shoulder with your clients and co-workers. But wait, somehow the story gets even worse…

Just over halfway through the flight, all the coffee in my stomach feels like it's percolating its way down into my lower intestine. I

Gummy Bears From Hell

hunker down and try and focus on other things. What feels like an hour, but probably isn't more than twenty minutes, passes. We then enter what turns out to be pretty violent turbulence. With each bounce, I have to fight my body, trying not to poop my pants. "Thirty minutes to landing, maybe forty-five" I try and tell myself, each jostle a gamble I can't afford to lose. I signal to the flight attendant and she heads toward me.

"Excuse me, where is the bathroom, because I don't see a door?" I ask while still devoting considerable energy to fighting off what starts to feel like someone shook a seltzer bottle and shoved it up my butt. She looks at me, bemused, and says, "Well, we don't really have one per se." She continues, "Technically, we have one, but it's really just for emergencies. Don't worry, we're landing shortly anyway."

"I'm pretty sure this qualifies as an emergency," I manage to mutter through my grimace. I can see the fear in her face as she points nervously to the back seat. The turbulence outside is matched only by the cyclone that is ravaging my bowels. She points to the back of the plane and says, "There. The toilet is there." For a brief instant, relief passes over my face. She continues, "If you pull away the leather cushion from that seat, it's under there. There's a small privacy screen that pulls up around it, but that's it." At this point, I was committed. She had just lit the dynamite and the mine shaft was set to blow.

I turn to look where she is pointing and I get the urge to cry. I do cry, but my face is so tightly clenched it makes no difference. The "toilet" seat is occupied by the CFO, i.e. our freaking client. Our freaking female freaking client!

Up to this point, nobody has observed my struggle or my exchange with the flight attendant. "I'm so sorry. I'm so sorry." That's all I can say as I limp toward her like Quasimodo impersonating a penguin and begin my explanation. Of course, as soon as my competitors see me talking to the CFO, they all perk up to find out what the hell I'm doing.

Given my jovial nature and fun-loving attitude thus far on the roadshow, almost everybody thinks I'm joking. She, however, knows right away that I am anything but and jumps up, moving quickly to where I had been sitting. I now had to remove the seat top – no easy task when you can barely stand upright, are getting tossed around like a hood rat at a block party and are fighting against a gastrointestinal Mt. Vesuvius.

I manage to peel back the leather seat top to find a rather luxurious looking commode, with a nice cherry or walnut frame. It had obviously never been used, ever. Why this moment of clarity came to me, I do not know. Perhaps it was the realization that I was going to take this toilet's virginity with a fury and savagery that was an abomination to its delicate craftsmanship and quality. I imagined some poor Italian carpenter weeping over the violently soiled remains of his once beautiful creation. The lament lasted only a second as I was quickly back to concentrating on the tiny muscle that stood between me and molten hot lava.

I reach down and pull up the privacy screens, with only seconds to spare before I erupt. It's an Alka-Seltzer bomb, nothing but air and liquid spraying out in all directions – a Jackson Pollock masterpiece. The pressure is now reversed. I feel like I'm going to have a stroke, I push so hard to end the relief, the tormented sublime relief.

"I'm so sorry. I'm so sorry." My apologies do nothing to drown out the heinous noises that seem to carry on and reverberate throughout the small cabin indefinitely. If that's not bad enough, I have one more major problem. The privacy screen stops right around shoulder level. I am sitting there, a disembodied head in the back of the plane, on a bucking bronco for a toilet, all while looking my colleagues, competitors, and clients directly in the eyes. "Pay no attention to that man behind the curtain!" briefly comes to mind.

I literally could reach out with my left hand and rest it on the shoulder of the person adjacent to me. It was virtually impossible for him, or any of the others, and by others I mean high profile business partners and clients, to avert their eyes. They squirm and try not to look, inclined to do their best to carry on and pretend as if nothing out of the ordinary was happening, that they weren't sharing a stall with some guy dropping his intestines out. Releasing smelly, sweaty, shame at 100 feet per second.

"I'm so sorry. I'm so sorry" is all the ashamed disembodied head can say...over and over again. Not that it mattered.

Gummy Bears From Hell

Tastes great…with a 74% chance of crapping your pants

Found these enticing little gummy friends at my local supermarket and bought a bag to help me hit my cravings on my keto diet....

On my walk back to the campsite where we were on holidays, I'll be honest, I ate the whole (small) bag. After all, they tasted great!

I'm now around 900m from the campsite and my stomach begins to rumble with an incredible pain.... It's a pain which feels like someone has inserted a hose up my rectum and attached the other end to a helium tank and turning on the gas to maximum. That's OK, I've dealt with gas before!

700m from home... the steps have shortened and I'm saying prayers for those walking behind me as the orchestra of my bum-trumpet begins its concert. I squeeze cheeks together and shorten my stride....

400m out... I genuinely feel that the pressure of the gas release behind me now is what's driving me forward. I'm not sure if I'm taking steps anymore. I'm essentially gas propelled. The gas, while painful, provides a mile entertainment but I start to be concerned about the wash I feel moving around in my stomach. I need to get to porcelain. This is getting real.

200m out... I start to squeeze tighter. I no longer trust that the gas is still the gas. My stomach is churning and my eyes are watering. I'm thinking back to the morning and whether my undies are in fact from my 'select' collection or whether I can sacrifice them. I'm unsure. I think they are the new Bonds briefs.... at $27 a pair, they aren't worth the single pack of gas gummies. I need to fight on.

100m out... I can see my wife, she waves and smiles...I can't pretend to smile at this stage. I'm in a complete stage of 'flex'... everything is tense. My stomach is singing baritone and my poor exit valve is under more pressure than the Australian dollar... Then I spy my 4yo son who has seen his daddy coming back... he runs at me... I immediately know I can't take the pressure of running cuddle from my little guy and change tack toward the camp ground toilets...

30m out... My son is 50m out and running to his dad... the toilets are 30m but they are static.... my stomach is far from static, I'm in pain, both from the gas build up and the incredible tension I'm forcing into my sphincter to hold the line... I'm at a maximum stride from the knees down, above that I cannot risk of a heavy gate.

10m out... my son and the toilet door look set to make a contest of it, I see my boy dig into his stride, I realize I can't go any faster and catch him as he jumps at me and I feel the rip of the pressure release.....

He asks "Daddy, why are you crying?"

Gummi Bears mate... Gummi Bears.

And don't worry about that running down Daddy's leg.

I pooped my pants mere meters from the toilet

Please don't buy these. Who reads reviews before they buy candy anyway? I wish I would have. I pooped my pants approximately 10 minutes after I finished the pack. I'm never having the "healthy" option again.

Still pooping….

Well, they were absolutely delicious going down but the aftermath of these gummy bears on my system will be felt long after. I fear I may be in a state of decomposition, the smells that are coming out of me can only be described as deadly and akin to rotting flesh.

In short, do not buy these - they will kill you and the gas you produce with kill those closest to you.

Gummy Bears From Hell

Not Safe for Humans

There has been lots of talk on the internet about sugar-free gummy bears and how they make you make shit like a madman. According to these detailed reviews, just a handful of the bears can cause an immediate evacuation of the gastrointestinal tract. There are 53 pages of reviews online, each one topping the last with a story of gummy-fueled diarrhea nightmares. "Gastric exorcism at 30,000 feet," a reviewer named I Like Cheese wrote. "Don't use the bathroom on a Delta flight. That stench is from me, seven years ago."

I'm no avid online shopper or reader of reviews, but I've scanned my share and have never seen anything close to the kind of in-depth reporting that's found for the sugar-free gummy bears. The metaphors are akin to something John Donne would have written after a particularly stinging shit.
"Gastric exorcism?" "Liquid razor blades?" I wasn't buying it. This whole thing seemed like a stupid internet hoax—an excuse for people to pen elaborate fictions about their somewhat irregular but ultimately harmless gummy bear-induced shits. The reporter in me knew what had to be done. I bought a few pounds of the day-glo bears at a candy store in Manhattan and found myself in the VICE offices late last Saturday night, shoving handfuls in my mouth, determined to find out the truth.

I camped out on a leather couch in the lobby. Leather seemed easiest to hose down if I didn't make it to the bathroom in time. The bears were still cold from being outside and the first few were tough on the jaw. Once they warmed up, the texture was everything we've come to expect from the manufacturer. The flavor was amazing, too. Lycasin, the sugar substitute that's supposed to be the source of the colonic unrest, tastes amazing. Splenda and other artificial sugars have nothing on Lycasin, aside from the alleged diarrhea part.

7:25 PM - One of the reviews mentioned that they had only eaten 20 gummies before their bowels exploded, so I figured that would be a safe threshold dose. I hooked down a handful. The first half hour felt close to that anxious period right after dropping acid, when you're killing time and waiting for it to hit. I snuck a few more bears as I waited. They really are tasty.

8 PM - A half hour in, I started feeling weird. I hadn't eaten gummy bears since I was 12, and I figured that I would have felt the same after eating any fist-sized glob of gelatin. Meredith—the photographer who encouraged VICE to test these gummies in the first place (thanks, Meredith!)—brought over a trash bin. I started spitting out thick, red loogies. A few times I felt like yakking up the gummy bears, but I forced myself to keep them inside. If those bears wanted out, they'd have to find another way.

8:21 PM - Something felt wrong. Very wrong. But the bears were too good to quit. I kept eating.

8:40 PM - Gassy. An adamant voice in the back of my head kept telling me, "Slow and steady. Push things out too fast and you might let more slip than you want to."

9:02 PM - Shooting pains had begun. But after two hours of eating the bears, I still hadn't made a mad dash to the bathroom. Maybe my theory was right. Maybe all the diarrhea emergency stories were exaggerated internet fiction. Another bonsai kitten hoax. How mistaken I was!

9:15 PM - There's a movie called *Devil's Due* in theaters right now. In its trailer, there's a quick shot of a woman napping on a couch as something starts to force its way up from inside her belly. I felt like this was happening to me. The bears were gnawing at my stomach lining. I started to think this dumb stunt could actually cause serious damage.

9:30 PM - The office's night security guard walked by a few times to check on me and Meredith. By this point, I'd lost my ability to communicate clearly. My sentences came out fractured and punctuated with groans. The guard didn't seem particularly surprised that this was happening.

10:12 PM - A friend of mine asked if he could swing by and check on me. I stood up for the first time in an hour and gravity started to take hold. I just about let loose of everything I had inside me as I opened the door to let him in the office.

10:26 PM - The beginning of the end. The bears opened my lower pod bay door and a gummy hell sprang forth. I made it to the toilet,

Gummy Bears From Hell

just barely. My watery shit looked like a blend of bile and egg flower soup.

With all attempts at modesty destroyed, I allowed Meredith and my buddy to follow me into the bathroom. He shied away, but Meredith came in like a pro, knowing what kind of massacre she was walking into.

10:47 PM - Exhausted and drained of all liquid, I hobbled home, but the need to shit out all my water weight hadn't gone away. It took every ounce of my being not to shit my pants on the corner of Manhattan and Norman Avenues in Greenpoint, Brooklyn. My rectum put on a star performance.

11:00 PM - I crawled into bed, shaking and dehydrated. At least I got to the bottom of the Gummy Bear mystery. I ate the bears so the world wouldn't have to. I fell asleep with a noble sense of self-importance—and the faint smell of fruity shit clinging to my clothes.

11:49 PM - I dreamed a gentle dream. A well-groomed older gentleman led me by the hand down a long corridor. "The bathroom is right this way, sir," he said. "We keep this one for only our most important guests."
He stopped and pushed open a door, revealing the most magnificent and ornate bathroom I had ever seen. He smiled, nodded and quietly shut the door behind me, leaving me alone, and—

11:51 PM - I tore myself out of bed and ran toward the toilet, vomiting out of my asshole. Whatever happened in the VICE office was nothing compared to this. I dug my phone from the pocket of the pants bunched around my ankles, and fired up the voice recorder.

3:10 AM - I crawled back into bed after shitting for hours. I was a shell of a man, fingers pruned from dehydration. The wreckage I left in the bathroom was too much for my weak body to deal with. I left it for a roommate to clean up.

6 AM - My girlfriend woke up to get ready for work. She wandered into the bathroom, took one look inside, and stomped back to our bed. "We're never getting our security deposit back," she said.

Night of 1000 waterfalls

Well, I read the reviews...challenge accepted!

Final score - death bears 7...me 0.

You know how the online services present to you things that people also bought with your item...they should include some toilet wipes as a mandatory item with this.

My pre-colonoscopy meds were not as effective as the 40 bears I ate.

Why 40 you say? Well, I ate 5 and nothing...then 10. Nothing. Kept on going. Got a little cocky and ate 10 straight. Now, I'm thinking I've won! 10 more...sure, and 10 more.

It was at this point that I actually read the packaging. It actually says may have a laxative effect.

And here comes the night of a thousand waterfalls.

Don't do the challenge. I thought they were all making stuff up.

How do I end this pain?

Dear Lord,

Please accept me into your kingdom for I am unable to continue living this earthly life.

Take my soul immediately before my mortal body explodes with rotten gas and runny poo.

Amen

Gummy Bears From Hell

Like Distant Thunder

It all started at 6 in the morning. The night before one of my hunting buddies had bought these without noticing that they were sugar free. He's one of those guys always reading about the effects of food and dieting and stuff, and refused to eat them claiming they would make you gain weight. So he gave them to me.

I was out in the deer woods far from any toilet, or toilet paper. If I could go back in time, I would have run my friend over on the way, or made sure my parents had never met, because after just 5 or so of these hell bent demon possessed spawn-of-satan bears, I knew I should have read the comments before taking these off my friends hands.

It all started with a low rumble, like distant thunder, or the mating call of a rhinoceros. I was sure it would scare away any deer with in a 5-mile radius. But it didn't stop at that.

My intestines began to move inside of me like snakes after eating cherry bombs. My soul itself seemed to be working its way through my bowls. By then I knew I had to got out of that tree stand, but by then I knew it was too late. I made a break for it just as the sun began to rise. I ran like a madman in a way that I can only describe as a pregnant, ostrich sasquatch women. I had only made it a few yards when Lucifer himself shot out of me like a potato tied to a ceiling fan. I crumbled to the ground as I tried to rip off my extremely expensive no-scent camouflage hunting pants, but it was too late. I stayed in that spot for what felt like hours. My life flashed before my eyes, and I relived the time I caught my first bass.

I prayed to God to kick a satellite from the sky to crush me, but my cries for mercy were covered by the explosions of Satan still coming from my body. The stuff coming out of me would have caught fire if you'd struck a match anywhere near it.

As I sat with my tormented thoughts, I saw the biggest buck I have ever seen in my life - about a 12 or 14 point - walk slowly past my tree stand. A FLIPPEN PURFECT SHOT. I sat in a puddle of my own defeat trying not to suffocate on the fumes coming from the tainted turds.

After what seemed like an eternity, I managed to waddle back to my brand new truck where I had no other clothes or anything to clean myself with. The smell of my truck and the butt stains left on my once perfect seats will forever torment my dreams. I have gone through an eternity of air fresheners and nothing has worked. Whenever someone has to drive with me and they ask what happened to my truck, I tell them a really long story about how I delivered a calf in the middle of the night.

Miss Rona is shaking in her boots

My friend hasn't been practicing social distancing during the pandemic, so I bought him a bag of these gummies for his birthday. It's now been ten days since he left the house out of fear of pooping himself again. I'm not gonna say that sugar-free Gummy Bears are the cure for the coronavirus, but it certainly helps slow down the spread.

Stand by for jet propulsion

Did you hear that sonic boom? Yeah, that was me after three of these.

Gummy Bears From Hell

10...9...8...1

I was looking for a low calorie 'grazing' snack when I originally bought this product. Tastes fine. After my first enjoyment, I experienced something less enjoyable. That might have been something else I ate that day, so some time later, full of wariness and scientific curiosity, I ate some more just before leaving work.

1 hour and 30 minutes later, after retrieving the children from school, we arrived back at home.

During this time, the Gummi Bears, hereafter referred to as *The Fuel*, were being carefully processed in the fuel system of Space Ship Me. I can only assume that The Fuel is a highly advanced binary propellant because it is non-reactive and benign in storage and even during initial ingestion. But as with all binary propellants, when mixed with the complementary other half of the pairing, the results are highly energetic.

Turning my parental duties over to the capable hands of the Roku and widescreen TV, I proceeded upstairs apace, shedding unnecessary accoutrements as I could tell this cowboy was about to Go Rodeo.

Entering the Launch Facility (real estate agents refer to it as the 'master bath'), I approached the Launch Pad itself, a fine furnishing manufactured by American Standard. As it was handy to the direct path of travel, and to further the cause of Science, I stepped onto the bathroom scale and made note of my weight. I then configured the Launch Pad into the second receiving mode and positioned Space Ship Me atop the launch aperture.

All hatches closed! Exhaust fans to full power!
Sitzfleisch sealed to Launch Pad support ring! (It's a German double entendre, look it up.)
Fuel flow starting, easing open sphincter, commence count down!
10!
9!
8!
Whoops, 1!

Thrust built rapidly to the 100% rating of the nozzle. The exhaust thundered against the parabolic shape of the Launch Pad and reverberated back upwards, buffeting the structure of Space Ship Me.

I swear, if I had thought ahead to equip the Launch Pad with the kind of camera available for the Discerning Customer with Refined Tastes from a Discrete Retailer, you might have seen shock diamonds.

I know some other customers have thought that they might have needed seat belts, but from my dispassionate observation point, I could objectively see that I had not yet achieved Lift-Off. That happened on the Saturn V launches as well: they had to sit on the pad for a while at full thrust until just enough fuel has burned off to make the thrust exceed weight.

It's a long way to orbit, and I was in a hurry to get to the ISS, so the only thing to do was to go to 125% on the nozzle.

That's where things started to go wrong. Thrust increased, to be sure, hammering the porcelain, but the exhaust flow became turbulent. It was also becoming asymmetric. The signal came from below, "The engines canna take any moor, Cap'n!" (I have no idea why my arse has a Scottish accent.)

Fuel flow dropped off and the nozzle output dropped to merely 10%, with some damage to the combustion chamber.
But luckily, sitting quietly for about five minutes, The Fuel had regenerated enough pressure that I could make another attempt.

After about thirty minutes and several attempts, I had not achieved lift off, and Thank God, because I realized belatedly that I hadn't a plan for how to get through the ceiling and roof.

But the scale revealed that I had lost seven (7) pounds.

Gummy Bears From Hell

Change of life

These gummy bears will change your life.

I went to watch the new Batman movie a couple of days ago and decided to pick up some candy on the way. I wanted gummy bears but they only had the sugar-free ones. I decided to get some because "what could be the difference?" Turns out a lot.

During the commercials before the movie starts, I downed the bag. As soon as the movie started, I feel like I just pooped out molten lava and chocolate milk at the same time. As I run to the bathroom screaming and crying because it feels like the devil himself is coming out of me, I get a call from the theater saying after I was done in the bathroom they were escorting me out. Apparently, the smell was so bad in the theater that 12 people had passed out and 3 more threw up.

I got cleaned up and went home sad that I ruined my favorite pair of shorts and didn't get to watch the new Batman movie. As soon as I walked through the door, the house filled up with the smell. The smell was so bad that my fish died and I got evicted from the property.

DON'T BUY THESE GUMMY BEARS. THEY WILL CHANGE YOUR LIFE.

Excellent taste in small portions.

During one of the last of the 8 trips to the bathroom, I released such a large volume of gas that my external anal sphincter could not do its job, and remained open/relaxed, while about 4.5-5 seconds of gas was expelled. I've never experienced, or even heard of that happening.

It was so unnatural, that I had to check to feel if my colon had somehow passed through the anal sphincter muscle.

Fully weaponized Gummy Bears

The cramping started about an hour later, and soon enough I was as bloated as a balloon in Macy's Thanksgiving Day Parade.

When the rumbling started, I sprinted down the hallway and made it to the bathroom just in time for the Four Horsemen of the Apocalypse to stampede from my backside, laying waste to my home's septic system AND my will to live.

After three hours of a pelvis-shaking Gummy Bear assault, I was spongy and weak, surprised that I had any bones left. I cursed the manufacturer with the little strength I could muster.

AWESOME and EXPLOSIVE!!

The explosive gas let loose and to an explosive shart!!! One mile from home on my walk and it was a long mile back and I had a mess!! Fortunately for compression shorts it didn't run down my legs!! Now I had to hold the gas for fear of blowing my entire intestines out into my shorts!! I made it home and what happened then was like something out of Dante's Inferno!!!

My butt became an upside-down volcano!! Best to stock up on toilet paper and toilet bowl cleaner as you will totally spray the bowl and back of the seat!! I would no sooner get done and have to go again. When you get the urge to "go" you best be in proximity of toilet!!! I spent hours on the toilet.

Gummy Bears From Hell

Be Careful How Many You Eat!!

Flavor of these is great and watching my sugar intake: this is the answer. One word of strong caution. They are sweetened with Maltitol which is a sugar alcohol. Many people have gastro-intestinal issues with excessive consumption. I ate too many the first night. They are so good they are addicting!!

A few hours later my stomach started rumbling and felt bloated. Then the flatulence started!! WOW my butt was on continuous gas explosions!! That soon was followed by diarrhea from hell!! My butt became an upside-down volcano of very explosive diarrhea and I couldn't get off the toilet. I thought I was going to crack the porcelain bowl!! Not to mention I had a household of giggling people that were awakened by my explosive, noisy defecation.

As soon as I cleaned myself and got back in bed, I was running back to the bathroom. I didn't get much sleep that night!!

I found I can eat about 10 without much ill effect other than some gas. Eat more than that and you're gonna be doubled over, rocking back and forth on the toilet with exploding bowels!! Everyone is different so try just a few the first time and see how you handle them. You could really get revenge at the office or construction site though.

Be sure to buy Oxyclean, too!

"Be sure to also buy a tub of Oxyclean with this to get the blood and diarrhea stains out of your underwear, clothes, furniture, pets, loved ones, ceiling fans."

Do not consume

Never ever buy this cursed package of demonic bears. It was a pleasant day with my friends and I had decided to purchase what seemed like an enjoyable package of gummy bears.

Immediately upon opening, I caught a whiff of a very foul smell. Probably something similar to Larry the Cable Guy's unwashed behind. Unfortunately, my friends and I dove right in, ignoring the off-putting smell. We finished the bag then threw it out.

Later that night we attended my friend Big Buddy's party. My friends and I were in an intense cup pong tournament when all of the sudden, at the same exact time, we all made a dead-spring to the toilet. I was the lucky one to get in while my friends, on the other hand, had to unfortunately do their business in Big Buddy's woods. We all were occupied with this terrible situation that we had to forfeit the cup pong tournament.

By the time I had exited the room, everyone had evacuated the home including the host because of the horrific satanic smell. I went back to that area about a month later and all the trees in the woods were dead, along with all the animals because of my friends' loads. The home was also torn down for safety reasons.

Please do not consume these demonic bears and spare yourself and loved ones. And if you are reading this after eating the bears I recommend you go to a place where nobody lives. I will never forget what happened and the impact it had on me physically and socially. I am afraid some of the terrible particles released that day have seeped into my brain and blood stream. I have no idea how long I have.

Gummy Bears From Hell

hariHELLNO

It was a beautiful sunny Saturday morning. I had woken up around 10 am to find my water broke. I hurried and woke my husband, we climbed into the car, and we were on our way to the birth of our first child!! What a precious day it was going to be, or so I thought.

As I was laying in the hospital bed waiting to start the labor process, my husband ran to the gas station to grab me some gummy bears before it got too crazy. Little did I know that my piece of s*** husband was going to bring back the monster hiding inside the sugar-free Gummy Bear package. He ran in with the bag already ripped open, apologizing that he "already ate a few." I began snacking with not a care in the world, assuming that the biggest pain I would experience that day was giving birth. How wrong I was.

I began to feel stronger contractions and we received confirmation that I was ready! The miracle of my son was about to occur! Doctors and nurses organized themselves ready to grab him and at that moment, a pain stronger than the contractions themselves erupted my bowel area. I began to panic; was something wrong with the baby? Worse. Do you know the feeling when you know if you don't clench your cheeks it's gonna come out? Imagine having your legs spread across a hospital bed and KNOWING if you don't do something at that moment, a volcano would appear and erupt the entire hospital.

I tried to spare the medical team, but to no use. Those psychotic feral beasts destroyed my insides, raining toxic bullets over every single person in the room. I screamed as my husband left the room, vomiting uncontrollably. On the bright side, those evil bears pushed my baby right out. F*** you Gummy Bears. Not only did I s*** on my entire medical team and my husband missed his birth, I can also confidently say that those pains were far worse than giving birth. I wouldn't those on my worst enemy. When I tell you not to buy these, I'm telling you. They are crafted by the devil himself.

Just about the worst thing you could ever buy

The day was actually going great for once, and to ruined it all when the gummy bears from hell entered my once calm belly.

I decided to go the gas station to buy some snacks, including Gummy Bears. When I got home, I was already halfway through the bag and start to devour the rest of the bag. I started to mush up the last gummy in my mouth when my stomached did five backflips, two handstands, five back walk overs, four front flips, a solo dance routine, and the cheer routine from the Cheer Camp movie I watched when I was five. I sprinted to the bathroom my shin splints reappeared but luckily I made it because what happened next was TERRIBLE. The most horrendous goop poured out of my booty hole and overfilled the toilet. I am still recovering today.

Problems

The worst. I can't explain the pain I had while eating these gummy bears. So I get these for vacation, right? I ate these right before I got on my plane to go to Florida. That was the worst mistake of my life. As soon as I got on the plane, my stomach started grumbling. At first I ignored it, but then I farted and it smelt absolutely terrible. The thing is that everyone around can smell it, too. The person next to me clearly took one whiff of it and instantly started coughing. Next thing I know, I'm crapping my pants!

Gummy Bears From Hell

Very very bad

I got these because my uncle said I should. I brought them on the bus to share with a friend. I was fine in home room but when I got to first period…I let one rip. I thought it was a silent and not deadly one but it was the other way around. It was so wet the I ran out peeing myself, too. My thin black leggings weren't black anymore. I got to the bathroom and flushed at least 10 times. My butthole was ripped and the same was true with my friend. The school had to go on lockdown because they thought it was gun shots.

Help

I woke up one day to eat some gummies from my friend. I ate about 15 of these hell spawn bears. Them my stomach rumbled so hard and I started aggressively farting and it smelled so bad I almost threw up. I starting literally pooping myself. I had such hard diarrhea that my butt was on fire, it felt like I was pooping out hot molten pieces of lava. It felt even worse than Taco Bell.It was like the devil visited my bathroom.

Don't eat when not under a roof

I have had these gummy bears while I was hiking with some friends in the woods. An hour later my a** exploded and ruined my hiking shorts. I had to bath myself in a nearby pond trying to scrub my back with poop running up it. Will definitely purchase again.

Worst cramps ever please read before buying

Okay, first I need to say that I don't like gummy candy. But on my way to dropping my boyfriend off at work, he purchased a bag of them. When he first opened the bag. I thought it stunk but decided to have one. They were pretty good. We finished the bag off, with my boyfriend offering me the last three gummies which I accepted.

After riding around laughing and talking, he stopped mid-sentence and screamed "pull over," which I did. He immediately ran out the car into the bushes, which was unlike him. He started screaming "OH MY GOD I GOTTA TAKE A SH**" which made me laugh hard.

Not even 30 second later, I had painful cramps that were almost unbearable. I shut off the car and ran in the bushes with explosive diarrhea. Sadly, I sh** on my pants before I pulled them down. I heard shouting from where my car was parked "Is everyone okay?"

An older woman approached us. I told her my cat had jumped out the car and we couldn't find him she told us, "Oh poor thing. I don't think you'll find him out in these woods."

Her husband then said, "What the f*** is that smell?"

I replied, "I don't know, I smell it too."

He said, "It smells like someone died." Then he laughed as we chuckled out of embarrassment.

I know he knew we took a sh**. We then parted ways. About 2 minutes later, we ran for the bushes again. It takes 30 minutes to take my boyfriend to work - he was 20 minutes late which caused him to get fired.

I will never eat another gummy as long as I live, I got trust issues because of these gummies.

Gummy Bears From Hell

Performed exactly as advertised

To preface this, I will state that it is not good to upset anyone in the military supply network. This is especially true for a supply NCO (non-commissioned officer) who can be both creative and vindictive to those who earn his ire.

One of my biggest pet peeves was troopies who walked into the supply room and decided to go through things on my counter or desk. It is for these reasons that I purchased two bags of these sweet little revenge snacks.

I briefed my minions that morning that the snacks were to be unsullied by their hands. I told them that I would know and it would not go unpunished by both myself and the higher powers. They thought that I was joking but decided to not test my authority before my eyes.

With that said, I placed the bowl on the back part of the counter, just in reach of anyone loitering inside my supply room. The rules were posted for all to see when they came in. So they were warned. A large sign stated "If you touch my stuff, you will be punished." They decided to test me, I guess.

On this weekend, we were set to do a general cleaning and maintenance within the Battalion. My desk was rather busy as it was the Battalion Headquarters supply room. I was in and out of my office all day. However, I made sure to take the general measurements of the bowl of horror every time I came back.

Shortly before lunch, my unholy wrath began to strike. My supply room is one door down from the latrines and the row of male commodes is on the other side of the wall from my desk.

It was the first, but not the last.

It was initially heralded by the sound of Gabriel's trumpet escaping the sphincter of one poor soul. He hit the latrine and sounded as if he kicked the stall door open. For the next thirty minutes, I listened to the sounds of live humpback whales being butchered by a blind man wielding a chainsaw.

It was not long before another troop, this time a female, made her way to the latrine. She came from the indoor pistol range and had to cross in front of my door. I saw a pale-face woman with sweat streaking her face.

She was hobbling with one hand on the wall for support and the other on her stomach praying for just a little more time.

For lunch, I ripped into an MRE (the Army brown bag lunch) and listened to the ever-growing chorus of those who had so far snuck down half of my bowl of brightly colored Improvised Colon Explosive Devices. I was not sure if the other side of the building was seeing the same activity in the latrines, but the smell reached my door by the end of lunch. Good thing it was stations with an Infantry unit for the first four years of my career, so I was accustomed to bad odors.

One of the minions did not return from lunch, so I volunteered another to perform a possibly suicidal scouting mission into the male latrine in search of my wayward soul. He was there and had been there since the beginning of lunch.

By 15:00 (3 PM Civilian time), I was told that the unit was being locked down and there was an emergency meeting in the Battalion briefing room. I had a suspicion of the reason but attended as I was ordered to do. By this time, my bowl of gelatinous bowel howitzer ammunition was down to one-quarter full.

The meeting began slightly off schedule. At 15:22, the Sergeant Major walked into the room and looked as if he had just performed a three-day combat operation without sleep. The Battalion X. O. waled in not long after and looked as if he had been intimately assaulted by a rather insistent horse. I used all of my military bearing to keep from cracking a joke about calvary officers walking bow legged.

The Battalion Surgeon walked in and told us that there was a high chance that the unit had come in contact with a strange stomach bug. Roughly half of the Battalion was complaining of stomach cramps and explosive diarrhea. It seemed to mostly be affecting HHC (Headquarters) and C Co. (the company that was on the same side of the building with us – also the medics). Until the symptoms cleared up, we unit was on lockdown and c lean-up mode.

I went back to my supply room with the intent to bag up the remaining evidence of my involvement only to find that the bowl was missing. My minions were too wrapped up to notice anything, though. So, I began a search for the evidence that would probably land me in front of a firing squad.

Gummy Bears From Hell

The empty bowl was located in the admin offices. Someone found it and decided to liberate it from my supply room for the only group that I didn't want to upset. But they had already consumed the remainder of the biological weapons. As I left with the bowl, I heard the familiar sound of incoming fire from the senior pay clerk's desk, followed shortly by what sounded like Lamaze breathing.

That weekend, the entire building was cleaned from one side to the other. MREs were consumed in the hopes of plugging the torrential flood of liquid terror and every door and window was opened with fans going over a cup of Pinesol in every room. Three-quarters of the enlisted and half of the officers were hit with the mystery stomach bug and the medical supply room was in desperate need of more I.V. kits.

I don't know if the message got across, but it definitely was an entertaining weekend.

5 Stars

Help me.

So I pooped myself today

I've been making a conscious decision to try and start eating better. I bought these Gummy Bears to eat as a low calorie treat. When they first arrived, I sampled one and thought that they were pretty good.

The next day, I made the mistake I will regret for the rest of my life – I brought the bag to work. While working, I scarfed down a few handfuls over the course of a few hours. I must have had three or four handfuls. Almost immediately afterwards, I started to get terrible gas pains.

I work in a cubicle surrounded by other people, so I can't just let my farts fly out as they come. So I went for a stroll around the building, to discreetly vent the gas from my body as I walked down the hallways.

After I let a few of the farts out, I felt a wetness in my underpants. Panicked, I made a beeline toward the nearest bathroom. Sure enough, I had a full-on Hershey squirt in my boxers.

I sat in the bathroom stall for about 15 minutes trying to decide what to do. Meanwhile, people were coming and going. I was so scared that I started to sweat and shake.

I mulled over a few different plans for what seemed like an eternity. I finally decided that I would remove my boxers, flush them, and finish out the day commando style. I'm pretty sure that my boxers clogged the toilet. I got out of there so quickly, I'm not even sure.

While they were delicious, these bears cost me a pair of boxers and my dignity.

Gummy Bears From Hell

Death in a bag

I bought them on a dare, a dare that would prove to be the end of my already quivering gastric system.

I want to walk you through what happens when a human being consumes this modern-day edible chemical weapon.

Step One: When you bite into that gummy piece of laxative, you will experience the same level of taste enjoyment to eating that of a regular god-fearing Gummy Bear.

Step Two: After about twenty to thirty minutes, you will feel severe rumblings in your abdominal area not unlike Beelzebub blowing his horn from the depths of hell.

Step Three: Not only will your rectum resemble Niagra Falls, but you will be forced to contemplate the very purpose of life itself.

Five stars

I have been sitting on my toilet for five hours in excruciating pain. 10/10, would purchase again.

Sugar-Free

I weighed 189 pounds before I ate these. I'm now a skeleton.

Diapers needed

I was waiting in the Walmart check-out line and looked to my left to find a pleasant surprise – a pack of Gummy Bears somebody had dropped off and decided not to purchase. After trying to eat healthy for weeks, it was a sign, I needed those Gummy Bears! They needed me. So I decided to get them and ate the whole bag before bed, of course.

A few hours later, I woke up in the middle of the night because my bed was wet. I quickly realized that I was the cause of the spill. I rushed to the bathroom and the fire hose exploded, gushing for minutes. I cleaned up the mess and went back to bed, only for this unpleasant exposure to happen two more times during the night.

On my third date with the throne, around 5:30 am, a thought exploded into my brain almost as intense as my bottom half all night: those Gummy Bears must have been sugar-free bears.

After cleaning everything up and on my last set of sheets, I rummaged through the trash and found indeed that the whole bag of Gummy Bears I had eaten were sugar free!

The reviews are true. If you need a good clean-out, this product is for you.

With friends like these…

Tastes amazing. Butt hurts like none other coming out. Perfect for co-workers or friends.

Groan

If you want to spend 24 hours in the bathroom, eat a handful of these. What is so evil about them is that they come in the guise of cute little Gummy Bears. Run away…run far away…

Gummy Bears From Hell

Umm, smells like hell

This was the day that changed my life. I bought a bag of these delicious Satan snacks and they took me back to the past. They took me back to the day Pompeii erupted, instead of lava there was hot brown liquid feces exploding out of what could be the black pit of hell.

I was sitting on my toilet, sweaty, AF. It felt like I was in a sauna after drinking Vegi-free combucha while being punched in the gut by Arnold Schwartzenegger. The worst part was that I didn't have any toilet paper. I questions whether I should use my dog to wipe my sweaty crack of hell, but I'd rather shoot him before I put him through that hell-like place. All in all, 10/10, great gift, would buy again.

Yoo-hoo into a ceiling fan

Bought some elsewhere out of curiosity. Looked like someone threw a Yoo-Hoo into a ceiling fan. Maltitol should be banned.

Like my stomach was terrorized by a five pound pack of wild bears

I'm just going to start off by saying that you can try and not eat the whole bag, but eventually you will (because it is a delicious treat) and when you do, your stomach and sphincter will violently vomit deformed families of fused gummy bears, for what seems like a painful eternity.

Apocolypse

Lycasin: Latin for "Oh my God, my 220 pounds of internal organs, flotsam, jetsam, and offal are attempting to egress a 2.5 cm opening…all at once!!"

Movie treats

When I got these in the mail, I was quite excited to finally partake in their goodness. After all, I have had quite the cavity problem over the years, and I figured I had to do something to save my dentist the despair that struck over his face every time I walked into his office.

Nearly immediately after receiving them, I took the bag with me down to my home theater and ripped them open with a child-like craving. I popped them in my mouth one by one, careful to roll them around with my tongue and over and back and fro between my gums, lips, and tongue. I relished how soft and pliable they were, and the taste was exquisite. I could not believe that I was experiencing nirvana from a sugar-free product.

About an hour into the movie, things started to change and before long it was as if the gates of hell opened up in my room. I could almost swear I saw the hand of Beelzebub himself reaching forth from the depths of a gaping, red fissure that had become my rectum, claws and all scraping any which way they could to cause pain. I was doubled over in agony – if the weatherman had come on television that evening, I am sure there would have been a flash mudslide advisory warning issued in my home as that is exactly what had happened. My guts were on fire.

I ended up creating a tar-pit that Labrea would have been proud of. If it were not for my beautiful wife, I could have become quite entombed within my abode and fossilized in the times go by. I will say this, though, the manufacturer would not reimburse us for damages to our door when my wife came home and the brown flood of goop shot out through the narrow slit that she had created by turning the knob, busting it from its hinges into her.

These Gummy Bears are an exquisite deficacy.

Gummy Bears From Hell

Eat if you dare

I sit here writing this review at 4 am from my porcelain throne, a fixture that will become all too familiar with if you choose to eat these cute little bears from the pits of hell. I had to eat a pound of these little bastards after Man City must've thought they were playing American football the other week and lost to a team of Arsenal scrubs.

They were a bit chewy but overall, appeared to be nothing more than your average Gummy Bears. After about two hours with little more than some mild stomach cramps, feeling like one would expect from eating a pound of any candy. I'd begun to wonder if I'd gotten some duds.

Like the slow build-up of a Martin Scorsese film, however, those bears were waiting for their baptism scene to destroy my insides. It started with the cramping, very akin to doing 1,000 crunches and then being forced to hold the 1,001st crunch indefinitely.

Then came the initial "run" which opened the proverbial "flood gates." I'm over 30 and I'm beginning to wonder if these bears knew that and wanted to send me back to the can for each year I've been on this Earth to make me wonder why I'd ever been born.

In between gastrointestinal bouts of pressure washing the inside of my toilet from my anus, I lay in bed feeling as if someone were to punch me in the stomach, I'd explode and turn the walls of my bedroom into a soiled Jackson Pollack rendition.

To give you an idea, I'd spent $50 ordering a UFC Pay-Per-View only to willingly miss the last two to three fights on the main card because I didn't want to stray too far from my master bathroom. Thankfully for me (and my marriage) and fearing what might be coming, I convinced my wife to spend the evening at my sister-in-law's because, trust me fellas, nothing will be gained from your significant other experiencing this with you.

I'm no longer in pain but am still having to make trips back to my master bath on a regular basis. Eat these if you dare but be forewarned, they are not to be trifled with unless you want your toilet to be a staging ground for repeat fecal rehearsals of "the Red Wedding" from Game of Thrones.

Buyer beware

I thought the things people said about sugar-free gummies were exaggerated...what a fool I was. I write this in the hopes that future generations will break the cycle and never have to live through what happened to me in the harrowing hours that were to come.

That night I lay awake in bed, sweating, farting profusely and unable to sleep because I had to run to the bathroom every few minutes. The stench was incomparable to anything I had ever smelled before. It was like being anally raped in reverse.

To pass the time, I read the article about Hiroshima and Nagasaki on Wikipedia. Perhaps I felt a kinship with the victims of the attacks because it was a like a nuclear bomb had gone off in my bowels. If regular diarrhea is Fat Man and Little Boy, the effect of these villainous bears on my anus was Tsar Bomba.

At one point I recall Marlon Brando's monologue from Apocalypse Now and suddenly I understood everything. If I saw my worst enemy approaching a bowl of these, I would dive in front of it to save them from the horror of what I experienced on that black day. Woe be to anyone who fails to heed my warnings.

Gummy Bears From Hell

An Experience I'll Never Forget

This product quite literally changed my life. Never before have I had a bowel movement that convinced me I was hemorrhaging down there.

The effects are almost instant. I made the poor choice to eat these in my car while driving home from work. No sooner had I eaten a handful (which were exceptionally delicious) then my stomach did a triple backflip, and I nearly blew the seat of my car out the trunk. I sped home like a maniac and locked myself in the bathroom for several hours, much to the anger of my roommates. However, had they known the battle I was having on that ivory throne, they would have cried like babies.

To say I had explosive diarrhea is an understatement. It was as if a sewage pipe in my body busted. An eruption of volcanic proportions nearly killed me. A pyroclastic flow of feces, a hurricane of poop. I commend the genius who built that poor toilet, it weathered the storm admirably.

At the end, I was left with the job of plunging the toilet, cleaning the crime scene, and wallowing in a shame like I've never felt.

But after the grisly task was finished, an odd feeling overcame me. I felt.... liberated. Clean. Healthier than ever. I had lost 20 pounds through the experience, both from the sheer amount of excrement evacuated from my body as well as the liters of sweat that poured from my pores as I struggled through the strenuous pain. More importantly, I now had a new appreciation for the wonderful gift of life.

I cannot recommend these gummies enough. The reviews are true. They are laxatives of unparalleled potency. But they are also life changing... Next time I need a cleanse, or feel bogged down, or need a near-death experience to raise my adrenaline, I will gladly partake of these magical fruits.

I eagerly await my next journey with them.

Pretty sure my intestines died

So I purchased these two times: once for my boyfriend's house and once for my house.

Being the amazing girlfriend that I am, I decided to give these a try. I'll admit that the taste is awesome (all but the grapefruit) and I was happy thinking to myself, as I finished up the whole bag, that I am doing not only him a favor but also myself a favor by cutting back on sugar. Yay me for taking care of my body!

I could not have been more wrong! Holy sweet baby Jesus, the devil is alive! I would rather have paper cuts on my hands and dip them in lemon juice than to go through that again. I had a come to Jesus moment on the throne last night, praying that this isn't how it was going to end. Death from the inside (out) from a Gummy Bear.

Needless to say, here I am, writing this review, saying don't eat them for yourself, but pass them out at work and watch the fun.

Delicate digestion beware

I have never in all my life experienced so much robust gas ALL night long because of eating this product. Painful cramping and breaking the sound barrier till the wee hours of the Morning. I almost reached lunar orbit.

What makes it an even more memorable event is the machine gun poops I had all the next day. I looked carefully at the fine print on the back of the package and it reads "consumption may cause stomach discomfort and or a laxative effect. Individual tolerance will vary." So unless you want to play a mean joke on yourself or someone else, I would skip this one unless you really enjoy painful earth shattering gas for what will feel like an eternity followed by a day of explosive poops. Enjoy.

Gummy Bears From Hell

Life observations from a six-year-old perspective

Belches, farts and poops. Penises, butts, and boobs. All the great 'taboo' topics. Plus love, food, unanswered questions and more. Life observed and explained through the words of one very funny boy named Seth from the ages of 4 to 6. Enhanced by the sarcastic, snarky after-comments of his Daddy.

Says Seth is a collection of charming and funny true-to-life observations which will make anyone who has ever been a parent, a brother or a sister to laugh (and on occasion shoot the beverage of choice through his or her nose). Part $#*! My Dad Says without the nastiness and part Kids Say The Darndest Things, up-to-date in content and format.

All done in Twitter-length 140 character conversations.

THE OTHER STUFF PEOPLE ARE SAYING ABOUT SAYS SETH:

"Yes, ALL famous writers have an 8:00 bedtime. Go to sleep Seth."
Seth's Daddy

"I realize that at home, your Daddy writes down everything you say. But in THIS classroom, you have to write your own sentences."
Seth's First Grade Teacher

"Why do children with such small penises have so much to say about them."
The disgusted lady in line behind Seth at the store

Gummy Bears From Hell

MORE Life observations from one very funny kid

Seth is back. Older (by a year or two), wiser and with more comments on the world as he sees it.

DeathFarts.com is the second collection of the kind of things that can only be said by a child. Seth IS that child. Once again, his infatuation with body parts and functions show how much we take for granted…and how it all comes together naturally in a younger mind.

This time around, the topics are more varied, the comments and conversations are longer, and the vocabulary more interesting.

Co-Author and Seth's Daddy Gary Zenker once again adds colorful commentary and offers the other perspective on Seth's observations and questions.

Get ready to laugh.

All done in Twitter-length 140 character conversations.

THE OTHER STUFF PEOPLE ARE SAYING ABOUT SAYS SETH:

"DeathFarts? You named a book DeathFarts? How can I ever show this to my friends?"
Seth's Grandmother on his Daddy's side

"Seth is so funny, he makes me sit milk out my nose. Three times today. Chocolate. It was so good."
Seth's best friend in 2nd Grade

"OK, I'll say he's funny if he quits knocking me down and stealing my action figures at recess. There. Are you happy now?"
Seth's other best friend in 2nd grade

Gummy Bears From Hell

It's *NOT* What You Think

37 FLASH FICTION STORIES

GARY ZENKER

It's NOT What You Think Gary Zenker *White Lightning Publishing*

MORE Life observations from one very funny kid

A mother with a baby in tow robbing a convenience store. A class reunion with the high school bully. A chance encounter at a nude beach. A dream visit from a recently-diseased parent. A woman flashing her breasts at a fancy cocktail party.

What do these and thirty-plus more stories have in common? There's often more to the story and the characters that you would first believe.

In flash fiction format – 1,000 words or less – Gary Zenker weaves fascinating tales of characters and situations that are both familiar and unusual; normal and quirky; believable and far-fetched.

These stories will warm your heart, make you laugh out loud, shock your senses, bring you to tears, and most of all make you rethink about how people relate to and interact with each other in situations that range from the common to the odd.

THE OTHER STUFF PEOPLE ARE SAYING ABOUT SAYS SETH:

"A fun collection of flash fiction by the multi-talented Gary Zenker."
Tony Conaway
Co-author of Kiss, Bow or Shake Hands

"The author should have provided a roll of carnival tickets for the reader because each story takes you on a different ride. I would find myself excited to see what the next one would bring and became addicted to this book, could not put it down!!"
Donna T.
Amazon reviewer

"At least none of the stories are about me. I'm grateful for that, more than I can say."
Zenker's mother.

www.ingramcontent.com/pod-product-compliance
Lightning Source LLC
LaVergne TN
LVHW051601080426
835510LV00020B/3081